SOCRATES
IN SICHUAN

SOCRATES
IN SICHUAN

*Chinese Students Search for
Truth, Justice, and the (Chinese) Way*

PETER J. VERNEZZE

Potomac Books
Washington, D.C.

Library of Congress Cataloging-in-Publication Data
Vernezze, Peter, 1959–
  Socrates in Sichuan : Chinese students search for truth, justice, and the (Chinese) way / Peter J. Vernezze. — 1st ed.
     p. cm.
  Includes bibliographical references and index.
  ISBN 978-1-59797-672-5 (hardcover)
  1. Peace Corps (U.S.) 2. China—Social conditions—2000– 3. China—Social live and customs. 4. Americans—China. I. Title.

HN733.5.V47 2011
306.0951'090511—dc22

2011002684

Printed in the United States of America on acid-free paper that meets the American National Standards Institute Z39-48 Standard.

Potomac Books, Inc.
22841 Quicksilver Drive
Dulles, Virginia 20166

First Edition

10 9 8 7 6 5 4 3 2 1

To Sophie

CONTENTS

PREFACE

From June 2006 to July 2008, I served as a Peace Corps volunteer in China, teaching English at Sichuan Normal University in Chengdu. Beginning in my second semester, I facilitated a philosophical discussion group attended mainly (although not exclusively) by Chinese undergraduate English majors. My credentials for undertaking this latter activity consisted of fifteen years as a philosophy professor at Weber State University in Ogden, Utah, prior to entering the Peace Corps. The series of events that led me from professor to Peace Corps volunteer is, as the Chinese would say, *shuo lai hua chang*—a long story, which I won't bore the reader with since this is a book about the intellectual life of Chinese students and not the mid-career misadventures of an American academic.

Soon after these meetings began, however, I realized that the proceedings might be of interest to more than the participants, for what was emerging as the students debated topics as diverse as the status of truth, the meaning of life, the reality of fate, the definition of sanity, the necessity of religion, and the value of romantic love was a fascinating portrait of the Chinese mind unlike any I had been familiar with then or since in my readings about China. Indeed, despite the ever-increasing mountain of books dealing with modern China, very few focus on the intellectual as opposed to the economic, historical, or cultural elements of that society. One of the rare exceptions is Mark Leonard's *What Does China Think*, which lays out the various debates currently taking place in the think tanks of modern China. By contrast, this is the first work to explore the ideas and philosophical worldview on the ground in China today, providing a portrait of the up-and-coming generation of young Chinese in their own words. The moral, political, existential, aesthetic, and metaphysical topics discoursed upon offer the reader a distinctive look at the Chinese value grid from the inside. Readers will be especially surprised by critical discourse exhibited by the participants. While China is often presented as intellectually monolithic, these sessions demonstrate a level of candor that readers will find refreshing, as the students take issue not only with each other but also, occasionally, with their government.

It is hoped that the resulting portrait goes some way in leading us toward a more holistic understanding of China—one not obsessed with economics, nor focused on what we perceive to be the nation's enigmatic otherness. Sadly, we have already seen what happens when we fail to make the effort to understand a region of the world that is vital to our own security. No one doubts that a lack of knowledge or even curiosity about the Muslim world led our nation to numerous missteps both before and after 9/11. Although a great surge of interest in learning about Islamic culture ultimately developed, this unfortunately occurred after much of the damage had been done. What if this educational process had taken place earlier? Might some of the tragedy have been averted? By examining the Chinese people's values and exploring what they find meaningful, as this book attempts to do, we can pay heed to Santayana's warning concerning the dangers of not remembering the past. Indeed, I truly believe citizens putting forth a collective effort in this manner can lay the groundwork for long-lasting and mutual respect between two great nations.

The model for my project was Christopher Phillips, whose best-selling *Socrates Café* relates his experiences running philosophical discussion groups across America for average citizens. I willingly attribute any successes in applying this model to his inspiration while taking sole responsibility for any failures. As the reader will soon notice, I owe an intellectual debt as well to Richard Nisbett's *The Geography of Thought*, which I highly recommend to anyone wishing to further explore the Asian mind.

This book would obviously not have been written had not the Peace Corps offered me the opportunity to serve in China. The organization receives neither enough publicity nor funds but still continues to fulfill the mission President Kennedy set for it more than a half century ago, and we are a better country because of it. If you ask me, everyone in the organization deserves a medal, or at least a pay raise. But I would especially like to acknowledge Sandy Peng, my local Peace Corps supervisor/guru, for her kindness and wisdom during my two years in Chengdu, and Bonnie Thie, the country director.

Sichuan Normal University was my academic home away from home in China. I would like to thank Yang Tianqing, who was tasked with looking after the well-being of foreign teachers there, as well as my counterpart teacher Wang Jiali, who served as my guide through the sometimes enigmatic (at least to me) ways of the Chinese university system.

If a Peace Corps China volunteer is fortunate, he has a fellow volunteer on his campus. If he is especially blessed, he has sitemates like Spencer Brainard and Kristin Burke. Besides being regular attendees at the discussion and contributing to its success, both helped to make China a memorable experience for me.

By my estimate, hundreds of students sat in on at least one of the discussions, and I thank them all for making this amazing experience possible. For readability, I generally used the students' English names in the book. Here I would like to provide the Chinese names of those who were the most loyal members of the philosophical discussion group: Gong Liqin, Liao Xiang, Ling Qianfeng, Ma Lin, Qing Sun, and Tong Shuai. A final "China thanks" goes to my friend Li Juan, who made life in Chengdu much easier.

Back in the States, my parents, Francis and DeLoris Vernezze, and my sister, Mary Vernezze, supported me with material comforts during a crucial time in the writing of this work, while Deb Badger, Luke Fernandez, Pamela Hall, Greg Lewis, and Susan Matt provided moral support during the same period. Julie Vernezze added valuable editorial services.

ONE

What Am I Doing Here?

"What good is philosophy anyway? Doesn't science answer all meaningful questions?"

I have just finished my pitch to a group of about forty graduate and undergraduate students in English at Sichuan Normal University in Chengdu, China. Although the main duty of Peace Corps volunteers in China is to teach oral English at our assigned universities in Sichuan, Gansu, Guizhou, and Chongqing, we are also encouraged to develop secondary projects in order to connect with the larger campus community. This is what I am attempting to do right now, and it doesn't seem to be going particularly well.

The young woman asking the question has short hair and a serious look. The way others are nodding their heads suggests she has caught something of the zeitgeist of the room. She is seated in the front of a typical Chinese classroom, consisting of two rows of long tables that go back eight deep with chairs bolted into place and glaring fluorescent lights overhead. The Chinese classroom strikes most foreign teachers as unfamiliar and off-putting. It does not allow for the sort of intimacy of its American counterpart, where students can group together chairs to form the discussion circles that are the staples of Western pedagogy. Instead, the structure evokes and elicits one-way communication, which is the way most classes are, in fact, run. In short, the Chinese classroom is not a very friendly place, and this is not a very friendly question.

Actually, the idea to hold a weekly philosophical discussion group with my Chinese students is not one I can claim credit for. The inspiration came from

Christopher Phillips, who stole it from Socrates. I am not sure who Socrates filched it from. Believing that Americans had lost the ability to engage in meaningful discussion as a community and that ancient Greece—where the grand existential themes served as the subjects of plays attended by the entire community and the philosopher Socrates would wander the public square discoursing about virtue with his fellow Athenians—provided a much more desirable ideal of citizenship, Phillips went on a journey across America, visiting jails, hospices, nursing homes, and other public venues, setting up impromptu philosophical salons, which he called "Socrates Cafes," where ordinary people, with the help of a facilitator, could spend several hours speculating about questions of eternal interest to the human condition. This attempt to recreate fifth-century BC Athens in twentieth-century America not only resulted in a couple of unlikely bestsellers but also inspired people around the country to recreate Phillips's experiment in their own communities.

Could I pull off the same thing in China? Organizing regular meetings on such topics as the meaning of life, the reality of fate and the nature of truth would not only allow me to discharge part of my obligation as a Peace Corps volunteer. It would also, I felt certain, provide a unique window into the worldview of China's up-and-coming generation. There was only one problem: as evidenced by the comment, the students appeared to have zero interest in the prospect. In this way, of course, they weren't much different than their American university counterparts, who usually only take a philosophy course under the duress of the dreaded humanities requirement or to spite their parents. As a result of dealing with this attitude for a decade and a half as a university professor, I had become somewhat practiced at defending philosophy, even if it was not exactly what I had in mind when, in the throes of a mid-life crisis, I took a two-year leave of absence in order to fulfill a life-long dream to serve in the Peace Corps. Perhaps I should have just purchased a convertible.

Back in the States, I explain the value of philosophy to my students in this way: Philosophy literally means "love of knowledge." But we have to distinguish between different types of knowledge. At one extreme, there are objective truths, such as "the earth goes around the sun" and "2+3=5." Let's call these matters of fact. No one but crazy people disputes these things. (Of course, I know there are some philosophers who do, but I stand by the previous statement.) About such matters, however numerous or few they might be, there is no room for debate or disagreement. At the other extreme, there are areas of knowledge that are completely subjective, claims like "my favorite color is blue" or "I like pouring ketchup on myself." Let's call these matters of taste. These may not seem like knowledge claims, but in fact we do "know" our favorite color or preferred recreational activity. Indeed, if we don't know, who does?

If the world contained only matters of fact and matters of taste, life would be both incredibly simple and unbearably dull, for the unique human abilities to debate, discuss, and disagree have absolutely no role to play in such an alternate reality. Thankfully we have philosophy, which involves what we might call matters of value. Unlike matters of fact, philosophical issues do not admit of absolute answers that provide solid, objective truth in the manner of science. The proof of this is that we are still debating the questions put forth by the Greek philosophers twenty-five hundred years ago, while we have long ago left behind their science. But neither does it seem right to say these are just subjective like matters of taste. The best evidence for this is the fact that we simply don't treat philosophical issues like matters of taste. As I would tell my students in America, people blow up abortion clinics, not Baskin-Robbins.

Philosophy, then, comprises the gray area between objectivity and subjectivity, solid fact and mere opinion, and we enter into it every time we assert "that was a great film" or "this is an unjust war" or put forth any of the thousand and one value claims that make life interesting. Where would humanity be without meditation and deliberation about such matters? Would not a life without such examination, as Socrates had warned, be a life not worth living?

This is the answer I would like to have given. But it is a hard enough reply to follow if English is your first language. So I tried to make the same point in a simpler way.

"Science is great and wonderful," I say, not wanting unnecessarily to rile the audience. Despite a long tradition dating back to Confucius of emphasizing the humanities, today Chinese education, like its American counterpart, gives pride of place to math and science. Early on in their academic careers, students must choose either a math/science track or an arts/humanities track. Those who are capable are expected to choose the former, lest they send their mothers to an early grave. "Certainly, a society requires science in order to progress. But," I continue, "can science really answer everything? Can science, for example, tell us what a good life is?"

My student turns to the young man in jeans and a crew cut sitting next to her, exchanges a few words with him in Chinese and, after a slight hesitation answers, "A good life is a productive life."

"Well," I reply. "Is that science's idea, or is that yours? And how does science prove this?"

She grows silent, as does the group, which has stopped murmuring and text messaging long enough to find out how this verbal struggle will end.

"Well," she defiantly asks, "what does philosophy say about this?"

"You'll have to come next Thursday night and find out," I say. "This is going to be the topic for our first discussion."

TWO

What Is the Good Life?

There's a scene in the movie *Fargo* where a woman is describing to the police one of the suspects in a murder case. Although she had spent the night with the character, played by Steve Buscemi, the only words she can think of to describe him are that he was "funny-looking." I guess that would be my initial depiction of the gentleman who stands out most in my mind from our first meeting. About twenty-five-years-old, he had a bad haircut, ill-fitting clothes, and slumped slightly in his chair.

For the first half of the meeting, he sat quietly. Actually, for a while it did not seem like there was ever going to be a first half, much less an ongoing secondary project. Hatched the week prior, the plan for a weekly philosophical discussion group seemed headed for an early shower. By seven o'clock only three or four people had arrived at the coffeehouse outside of the south gate of campus. I was nervous. In order to secure the space for the evening, I had agreed to be liable for the purchase of 150 renminbi (roughly twenty dollars) worth of drinks, which would require the presence of between fifteen and twenty people. So not only my pride but a good chunk of my monthly stipend was on the line.

We had set up shop on the second floor of the establishment, one of three we would use over the course of the next two years. Its Chinese name translated as "joyful reading time place." Given the empty seats to be found there at most hours, the title seemed more aspirational than descriptive. But I liked the owner, even if she had gotten the better of me on the minimum-drink deal, and the second floor contained a large open area in the middle that was perfect for the sort of free-flowing conversation that I hoped would occur. On that first night I arrived early and, with the help of a few volunteers, had expectantly pulled together an odd assortment of couches and chairs until it resembled something like a circle. Now, sitting there forlorn and mostly unoccupied, the furniture looked about the way I felt.

"Not to worry," said Sophie, an ex-student who had helped me with the organizational matters. "It is just a little difficult to find."

Throughout the whole experience, her calmness in the midst of everything would always remind me of the Chinese story about the farmer whose horse had run off. "Good, bad," the man calmly replied to his neighbors' offerings of sympathy, "who can tell?" When the animal returns bringing with it several other horses, the man's initial skepticism about the catastrophic nature of the event seems justified, although when his son breaks a leg riding one of the new horses, his fellow villagers' concern resurfaces. Still, the old man sticks to his claim that one simply cannot tell whether an event will turn out well or badly. When the authorities arrive at the man's farm seeking conscripts for the army, his son's condition makes him an unsuitable prospect, and the neighbors begin to realize the old guy might be onto something. This was not the first time I would come to appreciate that Chinese stories are not just stories but come alive in the everyday lives of its people.

By seven fifteen, Sophie's confidence was justified. A group of about fifteen graduate and undergraduate students had filled the chairs and ordered their drinks. We were ready to begin. Most of the sessions would commence with my reading a brief introduction. I would usually outline how things stood on the topic in the Western philosophical tradition, throw in a smattering of related Chinese thought, and explain why the issue still seemed relevant today. Then I would open the floor for discussion and try to stay as much out of the way as possible.

Speculation on the good life in the West, as on almost any philosophical topic, goes back to the ancient Greeks. The word used in ancient Greece to describe the notion of the good life, *eudaimonia*, has no real equivalent in English. Translators use the term "happiness," but happiness as it is understood in America today is too trivial a concept to capture the meaning of eudaimonia. To begin, we think we can be happy one day and unhappy the next (though on reflection this may be a bit optimistic). But for the Greeks, eudaimonia was a much more stable concept. Once achieved, it was not easily lost except through great misfortune. Also, we think children and animals can be happy, indeed, happier than most of us. But the Greeks believed only mature adults in full possession of their moral and mental faculties can achieve eudaimonia. Anyone watching prime-time television would have good reason to doubt whether such individuals exist in contemporary America. The Greek word does have this much in common with the term "happiness." Aristotle claimed that everyone desired eudaimonia as the end or goal of life, and we might reasonably say something similar about happiness.

Interestingly, the same distinction between a fleeting feeling of bliss and a more permanent, settled state of well-being exists in Chinese. *Gaoxing*, *kuaile*, and *kaixin* are just a few of the terms used to describe the former, while *xingfu* is the consensus choice for the latter condition. Another interesting similarity between the Greek and Chinese conceptions of happiness is that both imply that the attainment of this desirable state is to some degree beyond the individual's control. Literally meaning "good gods," the term eudaimonia suggests that the person who achieves this goal does so with the aid of the divine, while the Chinese equivalent, *xingfu*, is explicitly related to the notion of luck. I would argue that this intuition (shared with the book of Ecclesiastes) represents a good deal more wisdom about life than we find in modern America, where the prevailing belief is that all that is necessary for success is a pair of bootstraps and the will to pull.

But though everyone might desire the same end, according to Aristotle people have fundamentally different views on what constitutes a good life. Whereas some covet honor and others seek pleasure or wealth, Aristotle himself believed eudaimonia consists in a life of virtue in conjunction with a basic array of external factors: a modicum of wealth, family and friends, health, and a good government, among other things. Indeed, it is generally agreed that on this topic Aristotle is a pretty good reflection of the worldview of the standard aristocratic Greek of the fourth century BC, refined and with the inconsistencies ironed out. In many ways, Confucius plays a similar role in Chinese culture, offering a depiction of the good life that dovetails with the life of the well-stationed nobles of his time. There is one significant difference. While the Aristotelian ideal had a relatively short run, Confucius's writings can be said to have shaped and molded Chinese thinking for at least fifteen hundred years.

But the question for tonight, I reminded the group, was not primarily histori-cal. Rather, we were here to investigate our own twenty-first-century conceptions of the good life.

"Family" was the first word uttered. It came from a woman I recognized from my initial meeting with the graduate students. On any given night, be-tween two-thirds and three-fourths of the attendees would be women for the simple reason that women comprised most of the English majors at Sichuan Normal University. She continued: "I think family is important. I cannot im-agine a good life without family." There was a nodding of heads and a sense of general consensus that was confirmed with a few follow-up comments.

Although the Confucian view of society is structured around five rela-tionships—ruler to subject, husband to wife, parent to child, elder brother to younger brother, and friend to friend—three of these five deal with family. This should provide some idea of the relative importance of family in the Confucian perspective. It's also worth noting that the character for "good" (好) consists of a combination of a figure representing a woman and a child. Certainly, much has changed over time. At least in name, there is no power differential between the ruler and subject in Communist China, and equality between husband and wife has been incorporated into the Chinese constitution. But the centrality of family—the beating heart of which is the obligation between parent and child—seems alive and well. It is enshrined in the second passage of Confucius's classic work, *The Analects*: "As for filial and fraternal responsibility (*xiao*), it is, I suspect, the root of authoritative conduct."[1]

That is, if you are not a good son or daughter, how can you be a good per-son? Care and respect for the parent is central to Confucian virtue. While Con-fucius offers his readers plenty of advice on duty to one's parents, my personal favorite is his claim that as long as your father and mother are alive, you should not journey far, and when you do travel, you should have a specific destination. I know my mother would have appreciated it if I had followed that one.

Evidence demonstrating the contemporary emphasis placed on these family ties was available everywhere I looked, from my twenty-something tutor's well-thought-out plan for her mother's retirement to my favorite government-sponsored Chinese television commercial. The latter, which I called the *xi jiao*, or "foot-washing," commercial, opened with the scene of a mother giving her young son a foot bath—a very popular activity for all ages over here and, I might add, one I enthusiastically recommend. Next, we see the woman, now in an adjoining room, repeating the ritual on her own elderly mother. We then cut to the son, who happens upon his mother in the midst of the above-mentioned undertaking. In the final scene, we witness the son walking from the bathroom with a basin of water and preparing to surprise his own mother with a footbath, both literally and figuratively taking his first steps on his lifelong road of Confucian responsibility.

As fate would have it, I had been asked early on in my time at Sichuan Normal University to present a lecture on filial responsibility in the West, part of a national campaign to promote virtue on college campuses. Although I had been a university teacher for fifteen years in America, I think this was the first time I had ever heard the words "virtue" and "college campus" in the same sentence. Despite an already heavy teaching load, I didn't feel this was something I could pass up. Reflecting on the foot-washing commercial, I began my talk by asking how many of those in the audience planned on having their parents live with them later in life. Almost every hand in the college-age crowd of several hundred shot up. Of course, it was possible that many in the audience may have been shamed into raising their hands. But the mere fact that *not* saying you are going to take care of your parent is a source of shame itself says something about the attitude toward one's parents that is prevalent here. Later in the talk, I passed out a list of various ethical transgressions—everything from telling white lies to adultery to theft to murder—and asked the audience to rank the various misdeeds from least serious to most egregious. Not taking care for an elderly parent was ranked by most as right below murder in seriousness, and above it by a few (I'm assuming in that case the murder contemplated was not that of the parent).

I was not surprised, then, to start off the evening with a series of comments that viewed family as central to the definition of the good life. But after several heart-warming testimonials, I had had enough. My role was not merely to serve as a sounding board for student views but to press them critically and, if possible, stir up a little controversy. This would always be a difficult task. Students seemed programmed to avoid open confrontation. Even when they disagreed with a classmate, they would find some merit in their opponent's view, declare he or she was potentially correct, or simply preface their remark with the infamous and overused, "there are two sides to every coin." Nor was this reticence to debate unique to my particular sample group. In *The Geography of Thought:*

How Asians and Westerners Think Differently . . . and Why, Richard Nisbett offers
a compelling explanation on why the art of argument never got off the ground
in ancient China as it did, say, in ancient Greece. In short, Nisbett argues, "It's
the geography, stupid." Historically, China developed as a series of agricultural,
farming-based communities, the healthy continuation of which required virtues
such as cooperation and harmony. Under these conditions, Nisbett argues, "We
would not expect that people whose social existence is based on harmony would
develop a tradition of confrontation or debate."[2]

By contrast, the industries that emerged in ancient Greece, also as a result of
its own diverse landscape, were occupations such as herding, fishing, and trade—
professions that required little cooperation. To be sure, agriculture developed in
Greece as well. But unlike in China, Greek farmers quickly became independent landowners and not members of a larger collective. As a result, they could
act much more independently and, without the requirement for cooperation,
Greeks could, and did, and do dispute freely—as anyone who has been there
lately will tell you. By contrast, travelers to the East universally acknowledge
the reluctance to engage in open disagreement in this part of the world. I can
certainly confirm that it took more work to generate controversy in my weekly
discussion group than in any corresponding gathering of Western students.

In order to shake things up tonight, I presented the group with the tale of
my counterpart teacher—the Chinese faculty member who served as my liaison
to the Foreign Language Department. After completing her master's degree,
she had been offered her current position at Sichuan Normal. At the same time,
however, she was being recruited by a college some two thousand miles away
near Beijing. Pulled by the lure of the big city, she was leaning strongly toward
the latter when mom weighed in. On the day she was due to sign the contract,
her mother showed up and would not let her daughter leave the apartment until she had promised to take the local job. My first thought upon hearing this
story was to ask whether her mother had talked to my mother. In any case, the
daughter's ambivalence presented a clear challenge to the seamless web of family responsibility and personal fulfillment that was being proposed. "Did the
daughter sacrifice her own well-being and personal fulfillment," I asked, "for
the sake of the family?"

In the face of a real-world example, the consensus began to break down. Although some proclaimed the daughter had indeed acted correctly in acceding to

her mother's request, a significant chorus equally loudly declared she should have accepted the job near Beijing. At this point, the unkempt gentleman slouching in his chair entered the conversation. He leaned forward excitedly and blurted out: "Confucius tells us that being a good son or daughter is the heart of good conduct. You cannot have a good life without good conduct, so the daughter did the right thing."

In truth, this was said haltingly and in broken English. The level of English ability at the discussion ranged widely, and this speech was certainly on the lower end of the spectrum. But ultimately, and with the help of some of the other participants, I was able to decipher most of his meaning. After this initial statement, he let loose another torrent that ended with, "*Gong, jin, hui, yi.*"

Although I initially thought he was once again speaking in broken English, it turned out he had abandoned any attempt to converse in the agreed-upon language for the evening and was going straight for Chinese. The words he uttered were prime Confucian virtues. I later tracked down the source of his quote, which he proceeded to give also in Chinese. The good person, says Confucius, is "gracious (*gong*) in deporting himself, deferential (*jin*) in serving his superiors, generous (*hui*) in attending to the needs of the common people, and appropriate (*yi*) in employing their services."[3]

I wasn't sure how the quote fit into the current conversation. Perhaps his reasoning was that the daughter was being neither respectful nor deferential. Or perhaps he had moved on to some other issue entirely. In either case, the list he propounded reminded me of an additional similarity between Confucius and Aristotle. Both thinkers focus their efforts on developing an ideal set of virtues, and a person is judged good or bad depending on the degree to which he succeeds in embodying these virtues. (And by "person," I mean "man." Another parallel is that for both Aristotle and Confucius, only men can achieve goodness.) Aristotle calls this model *ta agatha* or the "good man" while Confucius dubs him the *junzi*, or "exemplary person" as Ames and Rosemont translate it in their masterful rendering of *The Analects*.[4]

In addition to these four traits, the Confucian good person must refrain from intimidation, self-importance, ill will, and greed. Nor should he be anxious, confused, or timid. The opposite of the noble character is actually called the "petty" person, and Confucius has nothing but scorn for such an individual:

"Exemplary persons understand what is appropriate," he says. "Petty persons understand what is of personal advantage."[5]

In short, for both Confucius and Aristotle ethics is not primarily about behaving a certain sort of way but becoming a certain type of person. That is, whereas the trend in modern Western ethics for over five hundred years has been to focus on conduct as the basis for making moral judgments about individuals, for both Confucius and Aristotle it is a person's character that is primarily judged good or bad, not his deeds. Of course, individuals with exemplary character will invariably act in the appropriate ways. But there is all the difference in the world between telling someone to perform good actions and training them to develop a good character. An action-based ethical system would have us inform a young child that he should not hit his sister because, for example, it would have bad consequences (it would cause her pain) or violate a moral rule ("do unto others"). But a child being raised according to virtue ethics would be instructed that a noble person simply does not engage in this sort of behavior.

Virtue ethics, as the Aristotelian and Confucian approach is known, is simply not much in demand in the West these days. The last representation that I can think of in American popular culture was on a TV episode of *Leave it to Beaver*. When Beaver's bike is stolen, his father consoles him with the claim that although the person who filched it may not be brought to justice, he will nevertheless have to live with the fact that he is *that sort of person*. The character of the individual who commits it, not the consequences of the act, is the ultimate sanction. Contrast this with the last episode of the most popular comedy series of recent times, *Seinfeld*, where the failure of the cast to exhibit such virtues as courage, benevolence, generosity, or decency, as they laughingly videotape a robbery in progress, is reinforced by replaying a host of related flaws drawn from the show's nine seasons. While in the past the virtue of a television character could play a large role in our level of sympathy for the individual, the lesson of the last episode of the post-modern *Seinfeld* is that moral character doesn't matter. How else to explain the fact that for nearly a decade a show about some ethically challenged individuals had been the most popular program in America? Don't even get me started on *Jersey Shore*.

Indeed, the fifties of *Leave it to Beaver* may have constituted the last gasp for virtue ethics in America. The reason is that for virtue ethics to be successful, a society needs to have an agreed upon conception of the good person. This was certainly the case in ancient Greece, where the heroes of the Trojan War provided the appropriate role models. For China as well, throughout much of its recorded history a single ideal stood out to be emulated: that of the cultivated scholar-gentleman. But the situation in America today is certainly much more complicated. Is it Bruce Willis or Woody Allen that serves as the standard? Mother Teresa or Ted Turner? Confusion about the good abounds.

Something like that seems to be the case in modern China as well. Although the Confucian model dominated for more than fifteen hundred years, when the Communists came into power, they brought with them a very different notion of what sort of individual qualified as the good man. During the Cultural Revolution the unschooled peasant was the new ideal, and many of the intelligentsia were sent to the countryside to be "re-educated" by participating in manual labor alongside this new moral paradigm. With Mao's death, an egalitarian model still reigned, as aptly demonstrated by old photographs from the late seventies depicting the notoriously identical style and color of clothing. By the eighties Deng Xiaoping had declared that it was a glorious thing to be rich, and the rest, as they say, is economic history. One might well offer up as a definition of a modern Chinese what *The New Republic* once presented as the essential characteristic of Americans: a Chinese is someone who wants to be rich. Even my counterpart teacher—the one whose mother forced her to remain in Chengdu—began seriously considering leaving her position and moving with her husband to booming Shenzhen to seek her fortune in some other activity besides teaching.

Perhaps this multiplicity of views of the good explained the inability of this modern-day mouthpiece for Confucius to have much of an impact. Indeed, to most of the group he seemed an object of ridicule, his ideas as outdated as his clothes. But the finishing blow came from a young man who sat in a booth off to the side, away from the main circle of couches and chairs formed by students. Well dressed and well spoken, he could not have been more different from the first gentleman in philosophy either. "In truth, I find all this talk about virtue tiring," he began during a lull in the discussion. All eyes turned. "What I have been thinking about, and would like to get the group's opinion of, is how much money one needs for the good life. You see, I have been stuck on this issue for some time. I think about ten thousand yuan a month (about fifteen hundred dollars). What do you all think?"

A lively discussion ensued, concluding with the consensus that yes, one could live pretty well in Chengdu on this amount. Except for *The Analects*–quoting guy who had now gone silent, everyone agreed a reasonable income was fairly important for the good life. "Yes," said the girl who had started things off that evening. "You need money to take care of your family." We certainly touched on other topics, many of which would become subjects for future discussions: altruism, spirituality, fate, monogamy, and friendship. But nothing could convince our silent scholar to rejoin the conversation. And we never saw him again after that night.

THREE

What Is the Impact of Technology on Our Lives?

The topic for each week was usually chosen in the following manner. I would hand out a list with between fifteen and twenty questions, such as: "What is wisdom?" "What is art?" "What is reality?" "What is justice?" The participants would write one of these on a small scrap of paper. I would collect the ballots, and we would vote on each of their suggestions. At this stage, you could give the nod to as many choices as you wanted. We would then take the two or three most popular questions and hold a final vote to determine the winner.

Initially, I generated the list of topics myself. But soon the students were offering their own suggestions, although this was often a double-edged sword. While I appreciated their initiative, all types of ideas would emerge that were unsuitable for a philosophical evening. A large part of the problem sprang from misperceptions about what I was trying to do. Some people thought of the meetings as a lecture series. Others wanted to use the space to discuss subjects they found interesting, such as favorite places to travel. A few even seemed determined to initiate a group therapy session. At the start, I was constantly pushing back against this, explaining to them that the purpose of our sessions was not to teach them about things they didn't know but to prod them to think more deeply about what they thought they already knew. We would be operating with the Socratic model of mutual inquiry in which there were neither experts nor novices but simply a shared search for the truth.

In fact, what makes a good question for a philosophical discussion group is itself a topic for a philosophical discussion group. Questions should be of philosophical interest, of course, but this is not always easy to define. I suggested that the subjects of discussions be neither matters of fact (such as a political system) nor matters of taste (such as favorite travel spots). They were to be questions of value about which there were legitimate differences of opinion. Also, following a suggestion from Christopher Phillips's *Socrates Café* books, I recommended we avoid issues that immediately split the world into two opposing camps, for example, "Was the Iraq war justified?" or "Should homosexual marriage be legalized?" Although such queries are certainly philosophical, the problem is that the way these questions are phrased undermines the possibility of true dialogue. This is because individuals come into such sessions primarily hoping to see their side prevail and, as a result, don't really listen to those with whom they disagree.

Unfortunately, the guidelines were almost immediately violated. During the voting period at the end of our first session, one of few foreigners who participated, an American teacher, proposed as a topic, "What is future shock?" invoking the title of a book by sociologist and futurologist Alvin Toffler. Written in 1970, the work is amazingly prescient, arguing that technology is increasing faster than our ability to process it and warning of a variety of social ills that will follow in its wake. Although the student audience was intrigued by this esoteric term, I was a little uneasy. I was certain the ensuing discussion would consist of precisely the sort of top-down approach that I was trying to avoid: students sitting attentively while a Western teacher lectured them on some unfamiliar issue they did not at all understand. In my mind, the students were there to talk to each other, not merely to listen passively as they did most of their college careers, in classrooms that neither facilitate nor encourage discussion. My plan was to enter the conversation only to clarify points, raise difficulties, or move the discussion along. I never wanted them to view me or anyone as the final authority on the topic under consideration.

Despite my best efforts, a groundswell of interest developed in the topic. When it was voted in, I did not feel that I could thwart the will of the group without risking a backlash. But between the time it was chosen and the time we met, I decided instead—to the irritation of the teacher who proposed it—to transform the question in order to make it more suitable. In thinking about how to do this, I reflected on my own relation to technology in China. Take cell phones (please!). Calling and text messaging here are almost as ubiquitous as breathing. This is a particular problem in the classroom, where it is a moral victory if you can get students to set the phones on vibrate. It is no better with the public at large. I can personally attest that movie theaters and yoga classes are routinely interrupted, and that people see nothing wrong with talking or texting back in such situations. On another front, college students report computer use as their number one hobby. Although online pornography is illegal (at least I wasn't able to find any), a nationwide concern exists about addiction to Internet-based computer games. Cell phones and computers are only the most obvious examples of technologies that play a major role in China, as they do, of course, around the world. One way to pose the question in line with the guidelines I had proposed was what is the impact of all this technology on our lives? Were we better or worse off as a result? Put this way, I suddenly realized the question sounded vaguely familiar.

In 1750 the Academy of Dijon in France proposed an essay contest. No, it wasn't about mustard. The question was whether the advancement in science and technology had aided or hindered moral development. A then-unknown Jean Jacques Rousseau had the audacity to argue that mid-eighteenth-century France was morally worse off as a result of its technological advancements. His essay shocked the French intellectual world (no easy task then or now) and won the contest. How, I wondered, would his arguments stack up today? I decided to go back and reread his essay and see if his reasoning still had relevance.

First, Rousseau presents a historical survey, arguing that societies in which technology had advanced inevitably displayed moral decline. Would Rousseau today point out the numbers of teens having sex, the divorce rate, and incarceration figures (one in ten Americans by last count) in the United States, the most technologically advanced nation, as part of his evidence? Next, he argues that technology is often used as a way to perpetuate vice. Do online gambling and pornography prove his thesis? Even beneficial advances, Rousseau goes on to claim, when examined closely reveal, on balance, negative moral consequences. Technology has allowed us to traverse the globe as never before, but does this just take us away from our obligations to those at home? Does it distract us and make us less serious people? "The farther you go," says Lao Tzu, "the less you know." Technology has given us the twenty-four-hour news cycle and access to more information than previous generations could have imagined. But are we really wiser? Or do we just waste time surfing through a variety of meaningless websites? Rousseau laments that the time devoted to the sciences siphons our energy away from the cultivation of qualities that are truly important, such as patriotism, friendship, and compassion. Could not the same be said of the Internet? Finally, Rousseau asserts that technology creates a need for useless luxury. What would he have thought of cell phones, plasma TVs, Blackberries, laptops, and iPods? Does anyone really need an iPhone?

A degenerate nation wallowing in vice with no greater mission in life than to be distracted and buy the latest gadget: is this what technology has wrought? (Not that there's anything wrong with that.) Although I did not totally agree with Rousseau, I had to admit he made some good points. But I did not know whether these concerns about the value of technology would be shared by the students. China, after all, has the world's fastest growing economy, its size doubling every eight years since the late 1970s. By comparison, the U.S. economy has doubled once in this time frame. Were there any doubts in these students' minds about the effects of all of this development? In retrospect, I should have guessed the answer. There were a couple of topics that while to me seemed rife with controversy fell flat when presented to the group. One of these had to do with whether China should take steps to combat the increasing proliferation of Christmas celebrations in their country. (They shouldn't.) Another asked if transsexuals posed a threat to society. (They didn't.) In an economy that had been in shambles not that long ago, whose respect on the world stage depended in no small measure on its continued economic growth, it should perhaps have occurred to me that the notion that progress had a dark side would not go over big. (It did not.)

It started with the freshmen. I was introduced to Equal (his English name) when I gave a talk at the Eastern campus where the first-year students were housed. He approached me afterward, informed me that his major was teaching Mandarin to foreigners, and offered to help me with my Chinese. Although people were always doing this, it was usually with the hope of getting some assistance in English in return. Equal, by contrast, actually seemed sincere in his offer, prompting me not only to invite him to the discussion but also to promise to buy him a beverage if he would take the bus over to the main campus. He spoke halting but clear English as he peered ahead with an inquiring glance.

"Oh, Peter," he began, as if lecturing a naive sibling. "I do not think there is anything to worry about."

I was reminded of the scene in the movie *Annie Hall*: a fifth-grade Alvy Singer has quit doing schoolwork because he has learned that one day the sun will explode. His concerned mother takes him to a doctor, who consoles the young neurotic with the assertion that "this won't happen for millions and millions of years." Equal struck something of that same smug, self-assured tone in reply.

"Why not?" I asked.

"Look at all the good that technology brings us. We can talk with our parents when we are far away, arrange a meeting with our friends, or call for help if there is an accident."

"OK," I said and turned to the group. "Doubtless, technology brings advantages. But is there anything that concerns you?" I went on to list some of the claims made by Rousseau. After a prolonged silence, Tracy jumped in. She was another student from the Eastern campus. She had long, straight black hair and a stoic face that seemed never to crack a smile. Her English was very good and, more importantly, she had an extremely logical mind. She was especially good at what we in philosophy call the *reductio* argument, taking a point and following out its logical implications to show its absurdity. She was probably as close to confrontational as anyone who would join the group.

"If you are against technology," she suggested, "why not just move to the mountains?"

I could see this was going to be a long night.

"Look," I said. "I'm not suggesting you throw away your computers. But wouldn't you admit that Internet addiction is a problem here?"

Although everyone seemed to know someone who spent too much time on the computer, they assured me that technology was not the problem. By helping them to do research and keeping them informed, the computer was undoubtedly a boon. As in all things, it was simply necessary to find a balance. How about the environment? Weren't we essentially destroying the planet with cars? Certainly there was nothing balanced about the way technology was having an impact on the environment. China, I reminded them, was on a pace to become the country that sends the most carbon into the atmosphere. Unsurprisingly, this didn't go over big either.

"Isn't this being hypocritical?" said Tracy. "After all, America has been pol-luting for hundreds of years in order to develop, and now it wants to clamp down on countries like India and China for doing the same thing."

I tried another tack. Some in America argue that advances in medical tech-nology are allowing people to live a longer life but also making them more of a burden to society because the cost of their care is so high. But, they shot back, is this not just a sign of the decadent American lifestyle? In China, the old do not require such care. Rather than lingering in nursing homes the elderly remain active and are looked after by family. Nuclear weapons, anyone? Doesn't this technology threaten the world? Yes, they replied, but China's possession of these devices of mass destruction is necessary to assure its place on the world stage.

This was pretty much the way it went all night. Either they saw no problem with the technology, or the negative effects associated with it were simply part of the inevitable price to be paid for progress. In either case, no one here was throwing technology under the bus.

"So," I asked, "am I completely crazy in thinking that Rousseau has a point when he claims that technology has on balance made us worse off?"

Now, anyone spending even a brief amount of time in China will soon real-ize that people here will never tell you directly that they think you are wrong, nor will they openly disagree with you. It is all about saving face, the notion that it is impolite to embarrass or disgrace another. No matter how asinine they might actually consider your suggestion, it is never directly dismissed. Rather, you are informed that it certainly has it merits and will be taken under con-sideration.

No, I was assured. There was certainly something in what I was saying, and they would give it serious consideration.

FOUR

What Is a Good Marriage?

Not surprisingly, issues related to love and marriage were the focus of several discussions. While these sessions were invariably animated, it was not always easy to ensure that they remained philosophical in nature. In truth, the students would have been happy to come in and give each other dating advice, since most of them were there mainly to practice English anyway. It was my goal to get them to employ their linguistic abilities in a philosophically interesting manner.

For thinking philosophically, nothing is better than the "what is *x*?" question. Indeed, it was with precisely this question that Socrates began the whole discipline of philosophy in the West some twenty-five hundred years ago. Like all citizens at all times, Socrates' fellow Athenians considered themselves virtuous people (maybe not as virtuous as right-wing Republicans). But when Socrates would ask them the most basic questions about matters of morality such as "What is justice?" or "What is courage?" they would be positively stumped, and in a few logical moves he would have them contradicting themselves. In one famous instance, Cephalus, a respected elder, replies to a Socratic request for a definition with the assertion that justice is giving back what is owed. But, says Socrates, suppose you have borrowed a weapon from a neighbor, and he comes to retrieve it in order to harm someone. In this case, is it really just to return it? Rather than respond, the old man conveniently remembers he must depart for a previous engagement. Socrates seemed to have had this effect on people. Some like Cephalus were passive-aggressive in their resentment. Others were just plain aggressive, which probably accounts for the fact that he was put to death by Athenians in 399 BC for corrupting the youth.

The situation does not seem to have changed much today. Bill Maher lost his show on ABC for suggesting that the terrorists who attacked the Twin Towers might reasonably be considered "courageous." But in the hundreds of hours devoted to the discussion of his controversial statement, no one ventured to give a coherent definition of that term to disprove Maher's claim. Philosophy is all about justifying our everyday assumptions and scrutinizing with a critical eye what we think we already know. This makes the deceptively simple request for a definition constituted by the "what is x?" question the perfect place to begin a philosophical conversation. Just as we expect botanists to be able to define a flower, moral people should be able to say what a virtue is. Except that they often can't. And philosophers are able to demonstrate their inability in pretty short order—which is why they rarely get invited to parties. Keeping with this two-thousand-year tradition, most of the meetings began with a "what is x?" question. Tonight's was, "What is a good marriage?"

Still in search of an audience, the discussion seemed to be drawing mostly undergraduate English majors with a few recruits from other disciplines and a graduate student here and there. Adamant about limiting the number of Westerners, I advertised only in the Foreign Language Building, where the English majors had most of their classes, and would go out of my way to actively discourage Westerners from attending. Spouting off in a second language is intimidating enough without having to be surrounded by a room full of native speakers. For the first year, the only non-Chinese to attend regularly was my Peace Corps sitemate, Spencer, who served the dual role of breaking awkward silences and vouchsafing my various cultural claims about the United States to skeptical students.

One of the difficulties in facilitating was making sure the discussion stayed on track. It was depressingly easy either to wander off topic or to fail to deal with the proposed subject for the evening in a very critical manner. An entirely typical example came early on this evening in the form of a rambling discourse by a young man concerning his parents' recent attempt at matchmaking. Having just turned twenty-five, he was informed by his mother over the winter vacation that it was time to seriously start thinking about tying the knot. In actuality, there is a relatively small window for marriage in China. As in many other areas, it seems to follow the reasoning of the middle way: one must be neither too young nor too old. Although the minimum legal age for marriage in China is twenty for women and twenty-two for men, even more important than what is legally permissible is what is socially acceptable, and it is rare to find a Chinese girl who will profess wanting to marry (or Chinese parents who will want to see their daughter married) before she is twenty-five years old. Conversely, if that same girl reaches her twenty-eighth year and is still single, it's time for the parents to start burning incense at the Buddhist temples. Although the time frame is slightly more flexible for males, after a certain point both unmarried men and women achieve "elephant man" status in Chinese society, which might help to explain why the young man's mother had already started to panic.

Although he resented the intrusion into his personal life, the young man had to admit that the girl his mother had set him up with was a looker. Sadly, though, it turned out that the two had nothing in common. Her favorite activity was shopping, his was reading; she loved the night life, while he preferred a quiet evening at home; she had no interest in serious art or literature; they even had entirely different tastes in television shows. I couldn't help wondering, while he was running through this litany, whether they were heading for a *Green Acres*-type "fresh air/Park Square" dilemma (and if there might not already be a Chinese situation comedy about this). To top it off, on his grandfather's eightieth birthday the girlfriend had insisted on going shopping instead of attending the celebration, which is only slightly less of a cultural faux pas than pushing the old guy down a flight of stairs. Despite being shocked by this behavior, the mother was still counting on the match. "She likes her parents," he said resignedly. Whereas to an American, harmonious in-law relations would seem like an irrelevant consideration, in China discord at this level can be a real deal breaker. The way it was put to me more than once was that for the Chinese, marriage is not just between two people but between two families. As other members of the audience weighed in with similar stories, I became concerned that although the young man's saga was culturally revealing, it might not be all that philosophically relevant. Trying to bring his story around to the proposed question, I asked, "Are you saying that part of the definition of a good marriage is that it involves shared interests?"

"Of course," he replied. Interestingly, I had just discussed this issue with my British and American culture class. Always on the lookout for material to

supplement the bizarre textbook the university had assigned me for the class—
a textbook with a chapter on U.S. history that ended shortly after World War
I with the rise of the American Socialist Party and that offered such probing
review questions as: "Which one of the following is not a characteristic of Tex-
as? (a) cowboys, (b) oil fields, (c) rattlesnakes, or (d) gambling casinos"—I had
recently brought in a questionnaire by the Pew Foundation about American
attitudes toward marriage. In particular, the survey asked Americans to rank
the importance of a number of characteristics to a good marriage: faithfulness,
happy sexual relations, mutual interests and hobbies, adequate income, shared
moral values, shared chores around the house, and children.

Both the Americans in the Pew survey and my Chinese students ranked
"faithfulness" as the most important quality in a good marriage. Differences
emerged, however, further down the list. Although the Americans awarded second place to "happy sexual relations" (only confirming my students' view of
Americans as sex-obsessed), my two hundred or so Chinese students gave the
silver to "mutual interests and hobbies." One other major discrepancy was that
"shared chores" ranked third for Americans and dead last for my sample group
of Chinese students. Since over 90 percent of my students were women, I found
this last assertion especially surprising. But the emphasis placed on mutual interests and hobbies puzzled me the most, since like many of the Americans queried
I did not find this trait to be all that important to a good marriage. On the other
hand, I was divorced, so perhaps there was something in the students' claim that
since love will wear off and children will leave home, mutual activities are necessary to hold a marriage together in the long run.

But this made the direction of tonight's conversation all the more surprising. If mutual interests and hobbies are so important, shouldn't the group be
warning the young man off the proposed match? Yet almost to a person they
were in the mother's camp. How could that be?

By way of explanation, someone volunteered the following story. A disciple
asks his teacher to instruct him on the nature of love and marriage. "First, I will
teach you about love," says the master. He sends the young man into a corn field
with the instruction to find the biggest ear, stipulating, however, that he is to go
through the field only once and must make a single selection. As he starts his
search, the disciple notices that the ears are getting bigger and bigger. Hoping
to impress his master by bringing back the largest one, he holds off making a

choice. It is not long, however, before the size of the ears begins to diminish, and the young man realizes he has lost his opportunity. Filled with regret, he returns empty-handed. "This is love," the teacher tells him. "You keep looking for a better one, but later you will realize you have already missed the best." "What is marriage then?" The teacher doesn't respond directly but sends the young man out into an adjacent cornfield with the same instructions. Careful not to repeat the previous mistake, the student picks one medium-sized ear and saunters back. "Well done," said the teacher. "This time you had realistic expectations and made the best choice under the circumstances. This is marriage."

While I was wondering if I had seen this in a TV episode of *Kung Fu*, I noticed someone raising his hand. It was Lionel. This was Lionel's first meeting, but thankfully it would not be his last. There were a few people without whom the discussion group would probably have collapsed, or at least been a lot less interesting. If Sophie, with her talent for organizing and her enthusiasm, was certainly first on the list, Lionel was a close second. Although he was only a sophomore, his English ability surpassed that of most in the room, including the graduate students. He also had a penchant for tossing out references to famous figures from the history of Western ideas. To top it off, he seemed to abhor a vacuum and had no problem filling it with the sound of his own voice. This stood in stark contrast to the majority of students who, both in and out of the discussion group, were reluctant to volunteer an answer unprompted for fear of standing out from the crowd. As the Chinese saying goes, the nail that sticks out gets pounded down. In a setting where it was sometimes like pulling teeth to get participants to give their own views, Lionel's readiness to step up was often just what was needed to get the conversation rolling.

"I cannot agree with this story," he began. "Like Plato, I believe we are looking for our other half." He paused, smiling. "I know my princess is out there."

"Yes," said a girl from the back of the room. "Like Rose in the *Titanic*."

"Exactly," echoed Lionel.

If I had to name perhaps my biggest surprise in China, it would be the fact that my Chinese undergraduates had seen more American films than my American undergraduates, whose attention span rarely exceeded the length of the average music video. Not that the motivation on this side of the Pacific was necessarily or at all aesthetic. The students here simply realized that watching American movies was an excellent language-learning tool. Fortunately, the result of all this extracurricular activity was a shared cultural vocabulary to draw from during our meetings. The impact of this cannot be overestimated. For example, you can save a lot of time and energy in a discussion of what constitutes a good person if everyone in the room (a) has seen *Forrest Gump* and (b) believes him to be the model of a good person. In fact, both of these conditions did hold on most evenings. Of course, there is still a lot of philosophical territory to cover, for example, what exactly is it that makes Gump a good person? But the shared aesthetic experience provides an excellent foundation for discussion. So tonight, for example, rather than having to spend time attempting to decipher what sort of alternative view of love Lionel was proposing, by virtue of the *Titanic* reference we all had a pretty clear idea of where he was trying to steer the conversation. And fairly successfully, it seemed, for I could sense the collective attitude of the room moving away from resignation and toward romanticism.

"I'm curious," I asked. "Since you mentioned Plato, is there in China the concept of finding your other half, your soul mate?"

"Not precisely," volunteered Carrie, a petite graduate student who for all the world looked like she was fifteen. "There is the notion of *yuan fen*." As soon as she said that everyone nodded knowingly.

I looked around the room waiting for someone to follow up. "Could you fill me in on the details?"

"Yuan fen is a Chinese word that has no equivalent in English. It is used to describe two people who really click. Like there is chemical reaction between them. And this is destined; maybe it was planned by some supernatural power."

"And people believe this?" I asked.

Everyone nodded. *Titanic* girl added, "For example, instead of saying 'We two really click,' I can say 'We really have yuan fen.'"

"And there is another interesting usage," said Carrie. "When a woman has no inclination to stay together with a man after several dates, she can say 'I am sorry, we just have *yuan* without *fen*,' or vice versa."

"OK," I said. "I get the idea." In fact, I was pretty sure I had been told the Western equivalent of this several times. But there seemed to be a problem. Hadn't they all just been arguing that one should grab whatever corn that's not seriously disfigured, taking pains not to be too picky? But now en masse they were signing on to a concept of a soul mate, which seemed to completely contradict that image. What was up?

"Well," said Sophie, who was often the first to understand the logical implication of something I was saying, and sometimes the only one, "I think that we all want to find our soul mate, but we realize it might not happen. That is where the picking-corn story comes into play."

Fair enough, I thought; no logical contradiction there. Indeed, this picking-corn story might be getting more popular these days. A long-standing preference for male children has combined with China's one-child policy and technology for detecting the sex of the fetus to create the perfect storm for gender imbalance. Currently there are one hundred and twenty boys for every one hundred girls, or as The Beach Boys would sing it: point eight girls for every boy. In less than fifteen years, China will have thirty million more men of marriageable age than women. Of course, the preference for male offspring is hardly a Chinese trait alone. Recall Luca Brasi's line in *The Godfather*: "And may their first child be a masculine child." However, in a medically savvy, one-child society, this sentiment results in a cultural nightmare. True, sex-based abortions are illegal in China. But so is toxic dumping.

But again, we seemed to be straying off topic. About all we had gotten so far concerning the definition of a good marriage was that it required shared interests. All this talk of true love, soul mates, and bizarre harvesting practices didn't seem to be moving the ball forward. Playing devil's advocate, I decided to try to shoot down the one positive answer we had arrived at, suggesting that perhaps shared hobbies and interests were not that important.

"Have you ever heard the phrase 'opposites attract'?" I asked.

Although many were familiar with the notion, they didn't have an especially high opinion of it. Perhaps, someone suggested, it was a belief in such notions that was responsible for the high American divorce rate. To be sure, while China's divorce rate has risen significantly in recent years, it pales in comparison to America's (it's nice to know we beat them at something). Still, I was curious how much they understood about this aspect of American life. "Do you know what the divorce rate is in America?"

"Much higher than China," came the answer.

"How much higher?"

No one knew. When I told them one out of two marriages in America ended in divorce, there was a slight gasp followed by a knowing nod. I tried to explain that this statistic was somewhat misleading because some people married four or five times. Seeking corroboration, I turned to Spencer. But despite his verification, the notion of serial marriage wasn't exactly providing a positive view of my fellow countrymen. Still trying to find my way on this point, I asked why they thought the divorce rate was so high in America.

"In China, when people have affairs, they still stay together for the sake of the family. But in America, personal fulfillment is more important than family."

In any country, I guess, you don't have to dig very deep to find a stereotype. But here it seemed sometimes you didn't even have to stick the shovel in before uncovering a stash of hasty generalizations. Perhaps the one that was most pervasive was: Americans are individualistic and emphasize personal fulfillment while the Chinese subordinate their own interests for a higher good, be that familial or societal. Indeed, there are a variety of ways in which the Chinese I encountered saw themselves as fundamentally different from Westerners in general and Americans in particular (and by "fundamentally different," of course I mean "superior to"). This idea has even found its way into official government publications. *The Economist* recently offered up a quote from that page turner, *Studies on the Impact of the Olympic Games on Boosting China's International Status and Reputation*: "In sport, Chinese cultural values emphasize the spiritual not the material . . . friendship and not competition. This is completely opposite of Western cultural attitudes to sport."

This illustrates a type of chauvinism I was to encounter not infrequently during my time in China. One morning I was at the track studying tai chi with a small group in the hours before classes started. The teacher asked one of the Chinese students to lead the session. After refusing several times, she turned to me and said, "This is one way that Chinese are different than Americans. An American would jump at the opportunity to stand out. In China, we are embarrassed to be recognized." A survey I took of my British and American culture class concerning which characteristics they associated with Americans and which they associated with Chinese verified that my students held radically different views of our respective cultures. Americans were perceived as individualistic, self-reliant, and independent, while the Chinese saw themselves as primarily family oriented, collectivist, and conservative.

In truth, I am not certain that the Chinese are as different as they imagine themselves to be. Nothing short of waterboarding would have got me in front of that group, while the young woman eventually agreed to lead the class. But in

The Geography of Thought, Richard Nisbett provides a good deal of evidence to support the claim that there are significant differences between East and West. On the issue of individualism and independence, for example, he cites one study in which candidates are offered a choice of two jobs: one that allows individuals to gain acknowledgment for personal achievement and one in which no individual is singled out. Ninety percent of the Americans, Canadians, British, Dutch, and Australians surveyed chose the former while the majority of Asians surveyed selected the latter. Nisbett also invokes a number of surveys supporting the claim that the further West one goes, the more one finds an endorsement of independent values.[1]

I wasn't yet willing to concede the radical differences they were suggesting, but I wasn't sure they were wrong either. So I changed the subject, trying once again to get back to the original issue, "Are shared interests and hobbies part of the definition of a good marriage?"

Yes.

"But these are also an important part of any real friendship, are they not?"

Certainly.

"Then what is the difference between friendship and marriage?" I asked.

"Love," came the reply, pretty quickly.

"But you love your friends, don't you?"

A noticeable silence, and then, "I guess we have to ask, 'What is love?'" offered Sophie.

"And what is friendship?" added someone else.

They were catching on.

FIVE

What Is the Meaning of Life?

I am not sure how a discussion about the meaning of life morphed into a tale about a young Chinese student trying to save an old, drowning peasant. But once it got there, it seemed like a good place to keep the conversation, since it was obviously inciting passion. Unfortunately, the person who inspired the whole evening was nowhere to be found.

Li Jiang was a graduate student in linguistics and the last in a long line of tutors who suffered through my struggles with the Chinese language. Although the Peace Corps paid for our continued language study, and quite well by local standards, that did not prevent several lesser souls from throwing up their hands in despair at the prospect of trying to improve my language skills. I guess they figured their sanity was more important than money. Not Li Jiang. She had that old-fashioned loyalty. Or perhaps she just really needed the renminbi. In any case, she good-naturedly stuck it out until the bitter end, and any progress I made in the language I owe to her patience and good will.

I was not alone in this struggle. Chinese is among the most difficult languages in the world to learn, with studies suggesting that it takes nearly two thousand hours of class time to become minimally proficient. I did the math and determined that this would have meant twenty hours of classes a week for my two-year commitment. Although this would have been fine with me, the Peace Corps had other plans for my next twenty-four months. Besides not being able to find enough time, complicating my language study even further was the fact that the local dialect in Chengdu is only tangentially related to the standard Mandarin that most who study Chinese learn. This had the effect of making communication with the dialect-speaking locals next to impossible, thus adding another impediment to the language-learning process. Despite all of this, I don't disagree with one of my Chinese friends who, upon hearing me complaining for the umpteenth time about the innumerable obstacles to a foreigner, or *lao wai*, mastering her native tongue, was reminded of the unskilled butcher who constantly grumbled about the dullness of his knife. What is the Chinese word for touché?

Li Jiang and I usually had tutoring sessions on Friday. Since the philosophy group met on Thursday night, we would often start the Chinese conversation part of my lesson with a discussion of the previous night's topic. She would invariably provide a different perspective on the meeting, one coming from a much more traditional, conservative Chinese point of view than many of my students. But one Friday our conversation took an unexpected turn. She was obviously a little low in spirits, and when I asked her why, she explained that she had been preparing for a big language exam and was feeling exhausted and overwhelmed. We continued on this topic for what remained of the conversation period and then, just as we were about to turn to the textbook, she said, as she sometimes did, that she wanted to ask me a question. Usually this was an inquiry into American habits or a request for an explanation of some item in one of the American newspapers she regularly read. But today it came from an entirely different direction. "*Weishenme huozhe?*" she asked. I wasn't sure if I had heard her correctly. Literally this translates as, "Why life?" But in that wonderfully condensed Chinese language, which can say so much in so few words, the upshot of her question was, "What is the meaning of life?" She went on to explain that one of her roommates had raised the following point: "You go to school, find a job, get married, have kids, then they go to school, and you get old and die." The usual smile came off her face as she stared at me in a puzzled manner and said, "*Weishenme huozhe?*"

No doubt religious people would seize on this remark as evidence for the deficiency of atheism. If she simply believed in God and eternal life, they might say, she would not be asking this question. Logically, they would have a point. At a theoretical level, belief in the next world supplies an answer to the question of the meaning of this one. But practically speaking the afterlife solves nothing, and the proof of this is that plenty of true believers get at least as depressed as

Li Jiang. Take Utah for example. Besides being the most religious state in the union, my adopted home and ground zero for the Church of Jesus Christ of Latter-day Saints (or Mormons as they are more popularly known) leads the country in antidepressant use. So it is not clear that religion would necessarily have helped Li Jiang. Besides, although it is true that religious people score higher on the happiness scale than nonreligious, their self-reported existential satisfaction seems primarily related to the social support system that church provides. The Chinese emphasis on the family and their strong social networking suggests that the conditions for well-being are as much a part of the Chinese society as they are for any religious believer in the West.

But if religion could not provide the answer to Li Jiang's despair, could philosophy? In truth, the question about the meaning of life is one that every philosopher dreads because people want it answered like "What's the capital of Nebraska?" and the fact of the matter is that no "Omaha"-type answer exists for this one. Besides, these days philosophy is more about breaking down and analyzing arguments than it is about responding to grand existential questions. As a result, most philosophers are in fact pretty leery of doing the latter, and I am no exception. If I am pushed on this matter, as I sometimes am, I generally say we have to distinguish between the meaning of life in general and the meaning of my life in particular. I go on to add that while I don't believe there is any overarching purpose to existence, I do believe that each of us is tasked with making his own life meaningful, and that this is something we are all capable of doing. Actually, that answer doesn't usually satisfy anyone back in the States, and it didn't seem to be working on Li Jiang either.

Hoping her peers could provide some collective wisdom that I seemed unable to generate, I told her we would take up the issue at an upcoming session of the philosophy group. She seemed excited and said she would be there. In the meantime, I contemplated how Confucius would have answered her question. Fortunately, I did not have to speculate too much because Confucius in fact did answer the question. "From fifteen, my heart-and-mind was set upon learning; from thirty I took my stance; from forty I was no longer doubtful; from fifty I realized the propensities of heaven; from sixty my ear was attuned; from seventy I could give my heart-and-mind free rein without overstepping the boundaries."[1]

I'm not sure exactly what the hell that means either. But it seems to express the boundless self-confidence of a man who never doubted that life had a meaning.

Indeed, a healthy functioning culture does not question the purpose of existence. The culture itself has the meaning woven into it, so that it makes no more sense to speculate about the meaning of life in such an environment than it does to inquire about the color of the sky. It is only when things begin to break down and competing value schemes seem equally valid that speculation about the meaning of life takes off. This is why Stoicism—the first philosophical system in the West to ask Li Jiang's question—came into prominence as the ancient Greek world was disintegrating. However, with the arrival of Christianity, this cultural fragmentation ceased and a millennium and a half of relative ethical calm ensued. Nietzsche's announcement of the death of God shattered this consensus and ushered in the current regimen of self-doubt, medication, and psychotherapy. Although for most of its history the Middle Kingdom can lay claim to a type of value unity reminiscent of Christianity in its heyday, China today finds itself imitating the West not only in wearing Nikes, consuming Big Macs, and coming up with its own version of *American Idol*, but in following us on the road to self-doubt as well. Indeed, how could it be any different, with Confucius unread, Mao dead, and Prozac not yet in widespread circulation?

The conversation tonight began conventionally enough with a discussion of the merits of living for oneself or for others, egoism versus altruism.

"I think the true meaning of life is found when we are living for others," said a young woman who was either new or was speaking for the first time. She went on to explain that she was never happier than when she was taking care of her grandmother.

"I disagree," said a young man, also a first-timer. "We have only one life to live. We must pursue our own desires and interests. What are we here for? We undertake our education in order to get a job and raise a family. We must take care of ourselves." This was beginning to sound like what my tutor Li Jiang had concluded, though she was much less sanguine about the results of her reasoning than this young man.

"So," I asked him, "do we have any obligation to help others?" Parents, yes, said the young man. Others he was not so sure about.

"What if," said Sophie, who seemed to be reasoning even as the words were coming out of her mouth, "in pursuing our own interests, we in fact are helping others? Bill Gates made a lot of money on the computer, but his invention also greatly helped society."

"Debate," says Nisbett in *The Geography of Thought*, "is almost as uncommon in modern Asia as in ancient China."[2] Confronted with opposing views, the Chinese tendency leans toward "resolving the contradiction, transcending it, or finding a 'Middle Way.'"[3] Given this, perhaps it was no surprise to see Sophie attempting to eradicate the distinction between altruism and egoism by declaring that both had a claim on the truth. Although in general I am a big fan of the middle way and think that our own society too rarely goes in search of it—a shortcoming that explains everything from our incredible litigiousness to our obvious obesity problem (the Chinese are right about that one)—it was my job here to stir things up. In addition, I was more than a little troubled by the resemblance between the emerging consensus view and trickle-down economics.

"Does this really work economically?" I interjected, trying to drive home my dissatisfaction with this idea. "I mean, if we encourage egoism by letting people make as much money as they want, will this necessarily benefit the entire society?"

Put this way, I had a feeling I might be able to generate some opposition to the swift resolution of the conflict between egoism and altruism that Sophie had proposed—at least if my oral English class was any indication. One of my more popular lessons there involved teaching students about American political parties. Most of them knew that Bush was a Republican, but beyond that, their grasp of U.S. politics was pretty sketchy—not unlike the situation with my American students. To fill in the gaps, I boiled down the differences between Democrats and Republicans to three basic but, I would argue, accurate points: First, I told them that Republicans believed government should do as little as possible, while Democrats favored expanding the role of government to provide social services and correct economic imbalances. As a result, Democrats sometimes argued on behalf of raising taxes, while Republicans were more inclined to cut them. Second, Republicans tended to be more business friendly than Democrats, whose suspicions inclined them to favor regulation in order to protect the consumer. Finally, whereas Republicans sometimes used the law to enforce morality, Democrats in general wished to leave individuals alone to make their own ethical decisions. After presenting this description and fleshing it out with examples, I asked students to write a brief essay on which principles they favored. Although this is information the Democratic National Committee will never post on its website, the party of Roosevelt and Kennedy won the hearts and minds of over three-quarters of my Chinese students. Here are a few typical remarks:

"I agree with the Democratic Party's social policy to favor a more active role for the government to implement policies to correct inequality and unfairness."

"Everybody lives in our society, so that if we want to live in a better place, we should do something and contribute to our society. What's more, the money owned by individuals is limited, but if we put it together, we will have stronger support for environment, education, research, and so on."

"I think the government should do something to make sure the economy works in the right way, that there are not too many rich people or too many poor people, and they should not just leave it alone."

Obviously, there was no problem with the idea of spreading the wealth here, although this rejection of unbridled greed was in part a geographical issue. Western China is much less economically developed than the Eastern part of the country. In a nation where nearly two-thirds of the people still make their living off the land, one does not have to travel far in order to discover a great disparity between rich and poor. Moreover, the students had their own reasons to align themselves with those on the lower side of the economic scale. Not only did the majority of them come from families of modest income, but it was also the case that most of them were training to be teachers—an occupation that, if possible, is paid even worse in China than in the United States. Why side with an economic policy so obviously misaligned with your own interests as trickle-down economics?

My guess was that the philosophy group would feel the same way as my oral English students toward a Gordon Gekko–inspired philosophy. And if they did not think greed was good, could the rejection of egoism be far behind? But just as the sentiments of the group seemed to be shifting away from pure egoism, at least from an economic point of view, the drowning peasant entered the picture. It was a story that everyone seemed familiar with and that had apparently been generating a good deal of discussion on the Internet. The details were simple: having witnessed an old farmer fall into a river, a young student jumped in to save him but drowned in the process. The online controversy centered on whether this was a tragic waste of life or a noble gesture. Tracy had brought it up as a way to revive the flagging case for egoism. "If you think the meaning of life is living for others, then this young student had a meaningful life. But I do not think so. Think of all the unlived life. Think of his parents. Who will support them when they are older? What benefit was there in this action? How will he now contribute to society?"

Most in the room seemed to concur with Tracy. From a societal perspective, this conclusion certainly made sense, especially when you factor in the one-child policy and the fact that, according to their cultural belief, there was no heaven waiting as this young man's reward (if indeed he ever existed, which I was increasingly beginning to doubt). Even so, dissent emerged. Sporting a crew cut, Richard had an intense look and a serious demeanor. Easily the most eloquent student to attend the meetings, he had recently been accepted to the Purdue University graduate program in math but unfortunately lacked the financial resources to attend. Just as unfortunately, work duties would cause his presence at our meetings to be short-lived. Although like an ever-increasing minority of the Chinese population Richard professed to be a Christian, he defended the young man's heroic actions with the words of Confucius, not Jesus Christ.

"In traditional Chinese culture, this would not have been an issue," he began, as if speaking to a group of foreigners who had to be educated in the ways of his home country. It would become clear this was how he viewed his fellow students: unmoored from their own past and in need of an introduction. "In ancient times and even not so long ago, there was respect for the elders. Today, they cannot even get a seat on the bus. Like the West, we have become a youth-obsessed generation. The old don't count anymore." At least on this last point, I had to concur, having witnessed the just-described scenario more than a few times, not that America has anything to be proud of on this point. He concluded: "The young man was setting an example of service. Without such examples, without the desire to sacrifice, there is no hope for society." Richard would turn out to be the strongest advocate for China and its most vocal critic. He believed only a renaissance of traditional Chinese values would save China, although I was never quite clear how he squared all of this with his newly adopted faith.

In *Thinking Through Confucius*, Roger T. Ames and David L. Hall offer advice any Westerner attempting to understand Chinese thought would do well to heed: "In the project of comparative philosophy, we have no choice but to attempt to articulate the other tradition by seeking out categories and language found in our own tradition that, by virtue of some underlying similarity, can be reshaped and extended to accommodate novel ideas."[4] Just so, one way to make sense of the divide that was emerging in the group was to view it through the lens of a long-standing controversy between the two great theories in Western ethics: utilitarianism and deontological ethics. Associated with the nineteenth-century British philosopher John Stuart Mill, utilitarianism claimed that the good is that which brings about the greatest happiness for the greatest number of people. By contrast, deontology, whose most persuasive representative was the German philosopher Immanuel Kant, viewed consequences as irrelevant. Instead, one had to rely on moral rules (such as "never lie") that could be applied absolutely and without any variation.

Richard might have claimed to be coming from a Confucian perspective, but it was my sense that by adhering religiously (no pun intended) to the principle that one ought always to try to save a life he was expressing a rule-oriented Kantian position. This was not surprising given his Christianity. Kant's view, as has often been pointed out, is essentially a restatement of Christian ethics; his central ethical claim—act only on that maxim you can will to be a universal law—sounds suspiciously like the golden rule. By contrast, his opponents that evening were reasoning on utilitarian grounds, arguing that the positive benefits of saving the old man's life were outweighed by the tragic results for the young man's family.

We had reached an impasse. Although Richard was outnumbered, he was more than holding his own in argument. In order to move the conversation forward I thought I would try out a little of the middle way myself. Summing things up, I noted that Richard was arguing in essence that the boy's life was meaningful, because it was lived in the service of a higher ideal that looked beyond his own life, whereas the other side seemed to be claiming that the boy's life represented a loss for his parents and perhaps for the nation. Weren't both sides, I pointed out, rejecting egoism and assuming that at least part of what makes life meaningful is the ability to live in the service of something higher than yourself?

"What about art?" said Sophie. "It seems the artist lives for something beyond himself through the act of creation."

"But will works of art take care of you when you are old?" replied Tracy sarcastically.

Defiantly, Sophie responded, "You can take care of yourself if you are healthy. Even if I have a kid, I don't want him to take care of me."

"Let's back up a second," I interjected. "We seem to have agreement that a meaningful life has the characteristic of being lived for something beyond self, although you two disagree about which version of this life is superior. Tracy, you come down on the side of raising a child, while Sophie is advocating on behalf of art."

Interestingly, these are precisely the two answers that Plato presents to the quandary of the purpose of human existence in the *Symposium*. In that dialogue he concludes that all humans desire immortality as the ultimate end of their actions, but that this can only be achieved in one of two ways. At the level of the body we can achieve immortality by bringing forth children who, by replacing us, will assure in some way our continuance, while at the level of the soul we can create works of art that survive our death. I was waiting to see how these choices would fare with the group when Richard spoke.

"It's a simple equation," said the mathematician. "Family is higher than individual, country is higher than family, and God is above all."

"So the religious life is the most meaningful?"

"Yes."

Welcome to the new China, I thought. I had recently listened to Rick Warren, one of the most popular televangelists in the United States, discourse on *Meet the Press* about the necessity for China to have some strong ethical influence to serve as a check on the excesses of capitalism. Although he didn't come right out and say that China needs to adopt Christianity if it was going to avoid going to hell in a hand basket, the intelligent listener would be forgiven for coming away with that impression. Richard was not a singular case study. With the massive push of missionaries from all denominations making inroads in China, Christianity is becoming more of a competitor with traditional Chinese values for the hearts and souls of the people. If the spirited exchange that followed Richard's pronouncement is any indication, traditional Chinese values are not going to go quietly. In order to calm things down, I asked people to state their own religious views or lack thereof. Here is a sampling of their answers:

"I don't believe. Because, when I was young, my parents told us, 'You should rely on yourself.' I might pray, but in reality, you should count on yourself. My mother says, 'If you believe it, it works.' On January 1st, we go to the Buddhist temple and make wishes for the New Year. I don't know if it works, but we do it anyway."

"I believe in a presence governing this world. After studying science in school, it seemed to me the world was too mysterious. But I don't believe in a religious God."

"When I was younger, I went to church. The priest talked about how the human body was so complicated, it could not have evolved by accident. Now, I am not quite sure I agree. It is a step-by-step process. First a single-celled organism, then a reptile, and finally a mammal. I think for myself. So I do believe in something, a superpower. In *Forrest Gump*, they talked about how people in China don't have faith. But we do have faith, although we do not have religion. We have morality."

"I do not believe in God. They say if you believe, it works, but if you don't believe, it doesn't work. Sometimes, though, I believe that if I do not behave well, something will punish me."

"Descartes said, 'I think, therefore I am.' If you think God exists, then God exists for you. If you don't, he does not. Sometimes I believe in God, or at least in a power that you can't define."

"For me, religion is like group hypnosis. The stories of the Bible show God to be selfish. But I do believe in something. I can call it God, but it is not God. People say, the Chinese people do not have religion. This is true to some degree, but not in a really important way. For the Chinese people have morality. They have very strong beliefs about right and wrong."

"To tell you the truth, I never thought about this problem. But I think if there is no belief, then that is a problem for society. But for me, sometimes I believe, sometimes not. Our education system, though, teaches us that the world is physical. But this I do not believe. Before this year, I have not been to Sichuan, but I have been to Sichuan in my dreams. How to explain that physically?"

"When I was young, I thought this question was easy to answer. Now I am not so sure. When there is some problem, I think, maybe God arranges this. My father and mother don't believe in God, don't believe in Buddha. But they tell me to worship the ancestors and ask for their help. I think this is very strange."

"I don't believe in God. I think everything depends on our own behavior. Religion is a superstition from our psychological mind. I very strongly don't believe in it."

"You need to know that the reason so few people believe in God here is because of our education. We are taught Marx from early on, and that everything is material. But for me, I believe in God, at least when I talk about things. Not so much when I do things, though. When I act, I don't think about God. Maybe that is the way it is in the West."

As you can see, students were all over the place on the topic of religion, so that it is simply incorrect to speak of "the" Chinese view of religion. On this topic, one comes away with more questions than answers, which seemed to be the direction the discussion was heading anyway. Thankfully, more students were beginning to feel comfortable with not having everything spelled out by the end of the evening. It had taken a while to reach this state. At the first couple of sessions, many expressed a desire for me to provide a specific answer to the evening's question. When I told them not only did I not have an answer but that this was not the point of the discussions, more than a few walked out and never returned.

As for Li Jiang, I told her about the discussion at our next tutoring session. But by then she had passed the exam and no longer seemed very interested.

SIX

What Is a Hero?

The choice of a topic for the following week was invariably an angst-filled moment for me. As the final votes were tallied, all I could do was hold my breath and hope the issue selected had some connection to the world of philosophy. In part this was my own fault. Although I usually provided the group with a list of standard philosophical questions from which they could decide, I also gave them the opportunity to submit their own ideas for consideration, with the following stipulation: unless the topic had been around for more than two thousand years, it probably was not an appropriate subject for our discussion.

This was not as onerous a burden as it might sound. Any reasonably interesting or thoughtful topic probably fits this description. Indeed, a quick survey of our weekly choices—truth, beauty, love, friendship, sanity—confirms that for the most part we stayed within this parameter. Even issues that seemed to be purely the product of contemporary events—such as the Tibet protests or the nature of our obligation during the Sichuan earthquake—in fact had ancient ancestors. In the *Crito*, Socrates had discussed the relation between the individual and the state, and of course Christ had a few things to say about our responsibility to fellow humans. But all the guidance in the world could not prevent some off-the-wall ideas from emerging as candidates for discussion. If someone insisted on putting forward an issue that seemed completely inappropriate, I could either take my chances by letting folks vote or simply veto it. I very rarely invoked veto power, however, relying instead on the group's judgment. But occasionally

I did not want to take the risk. For example, when Tracy suggested reality TV as a topic, I played the two-thousand-year rule card, though not entirely fairly, I admit, since someone could have pointed out that "reality" was a long-standing issue in the history of philosophy. Indeed, if I had been a little less jumpy, it might have actually made for an interesting discussion. OK, maybe not.

But I usually erred on the side of letting them vote. And though I occasionally regretted this, more often than not the choices they made were pretty solid, and a topic I found myself wincing at would in fact form the basis for a wonderful evening's discussion. Such was the case with the question "What is a hero?" When it was initially put forward, I did not think the subject particularly philosophical. I tended to share the view of my Peace Corps sitemate Spencer, who feared that we might be in for a night debating the relative merits of Spiderman versus Britney Spears. And to be honest, the names did come up. But all in all, it turned out to be a fascinating and very revealing evening.

Because of my initial skepticism about the topic, I took measures to ensure there would at least be some lively discussion by starting the conversation with what I thought would be a controversial issue. I had recently shown the movie *World Trade Center* as part of a campus-wide film series I had initiated on American culture. In the discussion following the screening, I had passed out paper ballots asking students the question: "Who was responsible for 9/11?" They had three choices: (a) Americans had no responsibility for 9/11, (b) Americans bore some responsibility for 9/11, or (c) Americans were completely responsible for 9/11. Given the contempt of America that was turning up in poll after international poll, the results that evening were hardly a surprise. About one-third thought America bore complete responsibility for 9/11, while the rest agreed that America had some culpability for the events of that day. No one, it seemed, was willing to let America off the hook, except me.

Many Americans not otherwise disposed to do so will find themselves overcome by an irresistible desire to defend their country when they hear it criticized overseas by foreigners. It's a gut-level reaction that seems to override any previously adhered-to value scheme. Although back home I had been a fierce critic of the Bush administration, over here I would not infrequently find myself engaged in dialectical combat invoking arguments that had all the political subtlety of a call to the Rush Limbaugh show. Philosophically, of course, this sort of confrontational approach makes no sense. As Socrates long ago realized, if you think someone is mistaken, the worst thing you can do is say, "You're wrong, stupid." Try using those words on a friend having an affair and see how well that works. It's not much more of a successful strategy in political discussion either. When the accusation is that America doesn't listen to other countries but instead acts without consultation from the international community, offering a knee-jerk response to the critique only solidifies this impression.

Rather than lecture at his listener, Socrates utilized a type of subtle inquiry intended to gently nudge him toward a realization of the tenuous nature of his own assumptions by asking a series of questions, the answers to which would ultimately land his opponent in self-contradiction. This is the famous Socratic method. When Socrates encounters a character named Euthyphro who is prosecuting his own father for murder—an act which Socrates clearly thinks is insane—he turns the tables by asking Euthyphro to teach the extraordinary knowledge that has allowed him to carry out such a bold action. It soon becomes clear that Euthyphro cannot take two logical steps without tripping over himself. In this way, Socrates does not discredit Euthyphro; rather, Euthyphro discredits himself. It is this method that I tried to invoke in the discussion after the movie. That is, rather than directly respond to the charges of U.S. culpability that night, I mainly asked questions such as, "Are citizens to be held morally responsible for the actions of its country?" and "Is it ever right to kill an innocent person?" My hope was that the attempt to answer these questions would get the audience to begin to wonder whether things were as unambiguous as they had previously thought. I'm not sure if I changed any attitudes that evening, but at least the conversation maintained a civil tone.

Believing that 9/11 would once again prove a flashpoint for discussion, I began the philosophy group with the question: "Were those who crashed the planes into the Twin Towers heroes?" In retrospect, I should not have been surprised at the failure of the question to generate controversy this evening. After all, the audience that argued so forcefully against America was a large group composed mostly of anonymous (at least to me) students who had simply turned out for a campus-wide screening. It made sense that this smaller contingent I was beginning to know quite well would be hesitant to assert that the terrorists who killed thousands of my countrymen acted in a heroic manner. So after an extended period of silence during which even Lionel did not venture forth an opinion, I changed the focus. "All right," I said. "Let me ask if you think they were courageous." Comedian Bill Maher had, of course, lost his television show by suggesting as much. What would this group think?

I could still sense a reluctance to answer the question. At this point, sufficient trust had not developed among the group to make them feel completely comfortable with speaking freely. This would come, but for now there were only a few students I could count on to give me their unvarnished opinion. Angelina was one of them.

"Angelina, what do you think?"

As if she had been waiting to be asked, she replied, "I think many people view them as courageous."

"That's not what I asked. Do you think they were courageous?"

After a few thoughtful moments she responded, "It seems, yes. What they did required courage."

"But what is courage?" shot back Marlene, who was obviously catching on.

The two provided an interesting contrast in styles. Slender, attractive, and very cerebral, Angelina scored points with the content of her responses, which were always extremely logical yet delivered calmly and with a smile that could cut like a knife. Short and stocky, Marlene resembled nothing so much as a pit bull physically and stylistically. She would fire back with a flurry of words that simply overwhelmed an opponent. All freshmen must engage in a month of military training before starting college, and I would often try to picture these students honing their battlefield skills. I had a hard time imagining some of them like Angelina surviving the experience, which involved long marches, little food, and less comfort. Marlene, on the other hand, seemed built for battle.

"That's not the question for tonight," shot back Angelina.

"True," I said, "but it still seems a legitimate one for the purpose of the discussion."

"All right," she sighed, weighing the fairness of my request while contemplating a response. "Courage involves overcoming fear."

"So," I added, trying to get her to complete her thought, "what fear did those who flew the planes into the Twin Towers overcome?"

"Obviously the fear of death," she replied.

Since the massacre at Virginia Tech had recently been in the news, I asked whether the individual who carried out that deed was courageous. She did not think so, arguing instead that he was too crazy to be afraid.

"But suppose that he was afraid and overcame it?" I asked. "Would that mean he was courageous?"

"But I don't think he was afraid; he was crazy."

We went back and forth on this a couple of times. Regardless of how hard I pressed, though, I could not get her to take the bait. In general, during the duration of the discussions I found it difficult to get students to comment upon an abstract proposition that had no chance of being realizable. Counterfactuals and hypotheticals—the staples of much moral argument in my Western classroom—were generally not well-received here.

Nisbett provides an explanation of why this might be the case. When Easterners and Westerners are given sample arguments and asked about their logical validity—whether the premises logically entail the conclusion—they do about the same if the arguments have what he calls "plausible" conclusions. For example, in the argument, "All men are mortal, Socrates is a man, therefore, Socrates is mortal," the conclusion—Socrates is mortal—is a plausible (in this case, obviously true) statement. Easterners and Westerners do about the same in picking it out as a valid argument. But consider the argument, "All things made from plants are good for health, cigarettes are made for plants, therefore, cigarettes are good for health." This has what Nisbett appropriately calls a "not plausible" conclusion. According to Nisbett, the Asian students tested were more likely to rate the syllogism as invalid if it had an implausible conclusion but was actually valid than were the Westerners.[1] The group's unwillingness to consider scenarios they did not feel plausible seemed of a piece with this reasoning. In both cases, the mind rebels against abstract possibilities divorced from realities. Far from being a logical flaw, this seems to constitute an admirable pragmatism.

"All right," I sighed, reluctantly abandoning this line of reasoning. "How many want to say that the bombers were courageous?"

Perhaps bolstered by Angelina's earlier assent to the proposition, a majority now seemed to be in agreement.

"How many think what they did was morally bad?"

Roughly the same number raised their hands. Here, I don't have to draw on Nisbett's experiments for evidence of an East-West divide, for I have discussed this same issue—whether the terrorists who flew planes into the Twin Towers were courageous—with my Introduction to Philosophy students every semester since the fall of 2001. Almost to a person, my American students refused to admit that the same act could be both courageous and morally heinous—even when the situation under consideration did not involve their own country. I believe a rather unlikely culprit lurks behind this discrepancy between my Chinese and American students' views of the moral status of the 9/11 bombers: Aristotle, the father of Western logic. As historians of philosophy have noted, the science of logic simply never developed in the East as it did in the West, and the impact of this resonates to the current day. Logic enforces strict rules of thought. One of these, derived from Aristotle, is known as the law of noncontradiction. Roughly, the claim is that "A is B" and "A is not B" cannot both be true at the same time and with respect to the same thing. For example, it can't both be raining and not raining at the same time and at the same place, a woman can't be pregnant and not pregnant, and so on. The upshot of all this is that the problem my Western students have in seeing the bombing of the Twin Towers as courageous may be as much logical as patriotic. To admit that this act is courageous is tantamount to claiming that the same action can have contradictory characteristics, that is, be both morally praiseworthy (because it is courageous) and not morally praiseworthy (because it killed innocent people).

A similar logical severity simply did not develop in the East, which is much more at home in the world of contradiction. In one study, Nisbett showed American and Chinese students two sets of proverbs: one group contained rather straightforward assertions, such as "Half a loaf is better than none," while the other group was constituted by sayings that expressed contradictory sentiments, for example, "Too humble is half proud." By now it should come as no surprise to learn that the Chinese students found the sets of proverbs containing contradictory sentiments more appealing, whereas Westerners had the exact opposite reaction.[2]

That a preference for contradiction (Nisbett's words) exists in the Chinese mind is certainly familiar to any reader of that other classic of Chinese thought, the *Tao Te Ching*. Although *The Analects* of Confucius has certainly had a much greater impact on Chinese history, the *Classic of the Way and Power,* as it is literally translated, is much more familiar to the West. Indeed, its eighty-one brief, elegant, and enigmatic chapters constitute one of the most translated works of foreign philosophy. Traditionally, authorship is ascribed to one "Lao Tzu" (literally meaning "old man"), who was supposedly a contemporary of Confucius, though in fact no such individual probably existed.

Dating from several hundred years later than *The Analects*, the *Tao Te Ching* is difficult to characterize briefly, though at least one of the major themes is the contradictory nature of reality. The most famous contradiction involves the claim that if you do nothing, nothing will *not* be done. Elsewhere it informs us that "being and not being create each other, difficult and easy support each other, the long and short define each other," as well as that "if you want to become straight, let yourself be crooked, and if you want to become full, let yourself be empty."[3] The symbol for all of this is the interlocking yin and yang, which has been variously interpreted but at least implies that reality consists of interconnected opposites that give rise to each other.

How, I wondered, would all this theoretical embrace of contradiction cash itself out here tonight? Would my Chinese students be able to accept apparently conflicting statements in a way their Western counterparts could not?

"Let's talk about the Rape of Nanking," I said.

The mood in the room immediately changed from animated and lively to quiet and somber. Mentioning Japan seems to have that effect here. For various chunks of the twentieth century, Japan not only occupied parts of China but committed numerous atrocities, among them what is popularly known as the Rape of Nanking. Between December 1937 and March 1938, the Japanese captured the city of Nanking and killed between 250,000 and 300,000 people, many of them women and children. Although it happened over seventy years ago, the Rape of Nanking was as raw and real for the participants tonight as 9/11 is in the minds of my American students. Quite simply, there is a different conception of time here. When asked whether the French Revolution of 1789 was a success, Zhou Enlai, the first premier of the People's Republic of China, famously said it was too early to tell; a little more than a century and a half was a bat of an eye for a five-thousand-year-old and counting culture. In China today, Japanese inhumanities during World War II are still a fresh source of grievance. Indeed, just a few years ago China lodged complaints over Japanese textbooks that seemed to them to gloss over Japanese wartime atrocities.

"Is it not the case," I continued, "that at the time, the Japanese viewed those involved in the Rape of Nanking as heroes?"

"Yes."

"But according to the Chinese they were evil?"

"Of course."

"Well," I asked. "Were the Japanese troops courageous?" This was something my American students had refused to acknowledge about those who flew the plane into the Twin Towers.

"According to the Japanese they were," said Marlene.

"I'm not asking about the Japanese," I said. "I'm asking about you. According to your definition, were they courageous?"

"Well," said Lionel. "If the definition of courage is overcoming fear, as Angelina has said, perhaps they were courageous."

"I disagree," said Angelina. "They were not courageous. They could not overcome fear because they did not feel fear. They were not rational. Like the killer in Virginia."

As soon as Angelina spoke these words, others jumped on the bandwagon relieved, it seemed, not to have to acknowledge the butchers of Nanking as courageous.

"I do not think they were crazy," said Lionel. "But I guess there are two sides to every coin." If I had a coin for every time I heard that phrase, well, I would have had a lot of coins. In any case, I was not sure how to score this one. There certainly seemed some resistance to ascribing the characteristic of courage to the Japanese under these conditions. But it was by no means unanimous, and Lionel had at least part of the room in his camp.

In any case, it felt like it was time to move on. But before I had a chance to change the topic, a hand shot up from the back of the group, and a voice I had not heard before issued a challenge.

"It seems we are not answering the question."

The voice was that of a graduate student who had attended previously but had not spoken. His English name was Pioneer, and it turned out he was in fact a graduate student in philosophy. Although he spoke English haltingly and one had to strain to catch his meaning, it was clear from his comment that he had understood the discussion. "The question for the evening is, what is a hero?" he began. "But it seems we are asking who are heroes, and not what the definition of a hero is."

I had to admit he had a point. In fact, and as I am sure he was aware, the error that Pioneer had identified was as old as ancient Greece. Asked by a young aristocrat named Meno how one can become virtuous, Socrates replied that they could not attempt to answer that question until they had first arrived at a definition of virtue. In general, Socrates believed that if you were going to en-gage in moral discussion, you first needed to define your terminology. This is as fundamental a point as there is in argumentative discourse, and yet it is one that is routinely overlooked in contemporary moral and political discussions. We will debate until the cows come home whether a particular tax policy is fair. Yet un-less you have a definition of "fair," how can you answer the question whether it is fair to give tax cuts to the wealthiest?

The upshot of Pioneer's rebuke was that if we were going to declare that some individuals were heroic, we first needed a definition of the term "hero." For all our bluster, we had not even scratched the surface of this issue. True, we had offered a partial definition of courage involving overcoming fear. But we had never explicitly linked courage to the definition of a hero, nor had we examined many of the complexities that go along with this understanding of courage. In short, we had some work to do.

"You are absolutely right," I replied. "Perhaps we can proceed in the follow-ing manner. Let's focus on individuals who are agreed to be heroic and see if we can find any common characteristics that unite them."

I thought I had some idea of where this might go. After lecturing on Joseph Campbell's notion that there is one story or myth of the hero that is found in all cultures, I had asked my culture class to write down the names of some of their heroes, hoping to illustrate the similarities between Eastern and Western views on this subject. It was an interesting list that emerged: most numerous were dead political leaders, notably Mao Zedong, Deng Xiaoping, and Zhou Enlai, in that order of popularity; second came entertainers, with the names of figures who had competed in *Super Girl* and *Super Boy* (the Chinese equivalent to *American Idol*) being the most prominent; third were sports heroes, with the hurdler Liu Xiang leading this group and Yao Ming a distant second, tied with David Beck-ham. The grouping was rounded out by a number of Americans, with Bill Gates garnering the most votes.

Like before, no consensus candidate emerged tonight, that is, until someone mentioned a name I had not previously heard. Lei Feng was a common foot sol-dier who by his own account desired to be nothing more than a "revolutionary screw that never rusts." Having studied the works of Mao, Lei decided to give himself heart and mind to the newly established People's Republic: sending his savings to the parents of a fellow soldier who had been hit by a flood, serving tea and food to officers and recruits, and washing his comrades' feet and darn-ing their socks after a long march. After he was killed in a tragic accident at age twenty-two in August 1962, his diary was reprinted and his simple life in service of the Revolution was held out as a model for all. Movies were made about his life, stills from these movies were turned into comic strips, and posters bearing his image were produced in staggering quantities.

Since we finally had a hero that everyone could agree on, perhaps we could begin to gather some characteristics and arrive at a definition. What, I asked, struck them as heroic about Lei Feng?

"His service to China," immediately came the reply.

"But there are obviously other ways to be a hero than serving China," I said.

They didn't quite understand where I was going with this, so I elaborated.

"If we are going to have a definition of hero, we will need a definition that applies to all heroes, not just Chinese heroes. So we might say that what made Lei Feng a hero was his service and sacrifice for a larger cause, and then define a hero as someone who serves and sacrifices for a larger cause."

"But what about a parent?" came the reply. "My mother is my hero." Many in the group espoused the same sentiment, calling some relative or other a hero.

"That works too," I said. "Since our definition of a hero is someone who serves and sacrifices for a larger cause, a parent or grandparent would fit if they do things for the well-being of their child or grandchild. In this way, they would be serving something beyond themselves."

Everyone nodded in agreement; it was time to pull the rug out. I returned with my opening gambit. "But couldn't we then say that the 9/11 bombers were heroes since they served and sacrificed for a larger cause?"

No one seemed able or willing to respond, so I did what any teacher hates to do: answer the question he is asking.

"Couldn't we point out that all of the other names we mentioned never purposely harmed anyone with their deeds? So that if being a hero involves the notion of service and sacrifice, it seems that not every service and sacrifice is the same, and we might reasonably disqualify those whose sacrifice actively harms others."

Although they seemed satisfied with this resolution, I was still a bit troubled. My image of a hero was, well, heroic. Perhaps it was my training in Greek clas-sics, but the protagonists of the Trojan War—Agamemnon, Paris, and Hector—

set the standard for my conception of the heroic: larger-than-life figures who performed deeds that surpassed those of mere mortals. I would also put literary giants, Olympic victors, or American presidents in this category: Hemingway, Jim Thorpe, or Abraham Lincoln. Even champions of peace such as Gandhi and Martin Luther King Jr. fit my definition. But a thoroughly average figure like Lei Feng, followed by a list of relatives? We seemed to be on a different page when it came to defining the heroic.

China certainly was not without an epic tradition in literature. Indeed, one of the best known figures in Chinese literature exhibits all the traits I identified as heroic. Granted he is a monkey, but no one's perfect. Possessed of superpowers including but not limited to the ability to turn his body hair into deadly weapons, leap for thousands of miles, and change his own shape at will, Sun Wukong, or the Monkey King as he is more popularly known, is no ordinary monkey. Interred into a mountain for his misbehavior, he is released in order to help guide a journey to bring the scriptures of Buddhism to China. Through four books and a couple of thousand pages of the sixteenth-century classic, *The Journey to the West*, he utilizes a myriad of magical abilities to fight off various monsters, extricate himself and his companions from countless sticky situations, and successfully return with the valued texts. So if the students had familiarity with a hero in the classic sense of the term, why was this ideal not catching hold tonight? I decided to push the matter a little more.

"According to one definition, a hero must accomplish something great or significant," I began. "This seems to be the case both in the West and in China." I went on to list all the Chinese examples I could think of, everyone from the Monkey King to Liu Xiang, the great Olympic hurdler. "But if this is right, it doesn't seem that Lei Feng would be a hero. Or mom and dad."

"My mom is my hero," came a defiant reply.

"So are there many heroes or just a few?"

"Many."

Silence. We were just operating with two different conceptions. I wasn't sure where to go next when Angelina broke in.

"It is like the Mariah Carey song," she said.

I had no idea what she was talking about, I told her, though everyone else apparently did.

"The song 'Hero.'"

When I confessed to barely knowing who Mariah Carey was and to complete ignorance of her music, it was if I had told Angelina that I did not know the capital of the United States. Not know Mariah Carey? Was I really an American? Undaunted, she pulled out a piece of paper containing the lyrics and read them. I can't recall the precise words, but they had something to do with looking inside yourself when you feel things are hopeless and discovering a hero within.

So all of us were, or could be, heroes. Expressed in this context, this sentiment suddenly meant something different than it would have in America. There, it might imply that we could all get our fifteen minutes of fame, hit the lottery, and win *American Idol* in the same week. Here, it seemed to mean that merely living a decent human life ought to be heroic enough to satisfy one person. For some reason, I thought of the line from a Woody Allen film, *Hannah and Her Sisters*, in which he is trying to discuss with his father such profound questions as how an all-good God can allow for the existence of a Hitler. "How the hell do I know why there were Nazis?" replies his father. "I don't know how the can opener works!"

What I had in mind when I began the discussion were world historical events and larger-than-life figures, whereas they were purposing a much simpler, more realistic and realizable ideal. More can-opener-like, as it were.

Perhaps I would go and download the Mariah Carey song.

SEVEN

Fate or Free Will?

About the last thing I expected to be talking about in a discussion on fate was *Forrest Gump*. But perhaps I shouldn't have been surprised. As I mentioned earlier, it is natural enough for people from different cultures to use a commonly shared aesthetic experience as a reference point in conversation. And as shared aesthetic experiences between China and America go, it doesn't get any better than *Gump*. Indeed, if you put a gun to my head—or, since guns are illegal here, if you asked me nicely—I would have said that the Tom Hanks classic is not only the most popular but also the most beloved American film in this part of China.

My first realization of the popularity of *Gump* came in my British and American culture class. Thinking the film might provide an entertaining and not entirely inaccurate portrait of several important decades in American history, I suggested a group screening. To my surprise, many Chinese teachers seemed to have reached the same conclusion. Not only had most of the students already seen the movie as part of their education, but many had been so enthralled that they had watched the film a couple or ten more times on their own. I was curious. Why *Gump*? What was it about this film that accounted for their enthusiasm? The reason most often given by the members of my culture class was that Forrest Gump was a good man, as demonstrated by his obvious love of his mother and his care for the ailing Jenny. But they also pointed to the fact that, despite having been underestimated by almost everyone, this was a man who, through hard work and perseverance, had become a great success.

It began to dawn on me that many of my students might view their own country as a sort of Forrest Gump. Like Gump among his contemporaries, these students saw China as having much more traditional views about morality than its decadent European and American counterparts. In addition, China, like Gump, had been an outcast, having once been dubbed the "sick man of Asia." But just as Gump had ultimately achieved power and wealth through quiet, steady effort, so China, too, was beginning its own "peaceful rise," or what the Chinese call *heping jueqi*. Now I don't want to make too much of this aesthetic-event-as-metaphor-for-China. *Prison Break* was incredibly popular during my time in China, but I don't think it was because all those Chinese who watched the show perceived their country as a jail from which they wished to escape. Nevertheless, I don't think my Gumpian speculation is entirely off base either.

Indeed, this interpretation of the Gump story is of a piece with one of the most well-known and beloved Chinese fables: "The Foolish Old Man Who Moved Mountains." According to the story, an elderly farmer wishes to get rid of two large mountains that stand in front of his house and starts to dig them up, shovel by shovel. When his neighbors all laugh at this apparent futility, he explains that although the mountains will not be removed in his lifetime, or in his children's or grandchildren's lifetime, given enough time they will ultimately fall. Impressed by the man's dedication, the gods come to his assistance and remove the giant obstacles.

I first learned of the story through an article in the feature section of *China Daily*—the largest English language newspaper in China. A local student of English detailed his dismay at a foreign friend's reaction to the folk tale. Whereas to the young Chinese undergraduate it represented something profound about his country's spirit, through the lens of German pragmatism the old man's actions bordered on absurdity. Wouldn't it make much more sense just to pack up and move? Back and forth they went, the Chinese student defending the seemingly futile undertakings, the German friend rebutting him at every turn until, ultimately, the young advocate abandoned his efforts. Some things cannot be explained, he reasoned, they simply must be accepted. This is what makes a culture unique. Later, I discovered that Mao had used the story as the basis for one of his more famous speeches. To be sure, this sort of ceaseless effort against the odds is admired by Americans as well—witness Gump, or Gatsby. But just as I would argue that Chinese patriotism is like American patriotism in name only, being in fact of a much more intense variety, so I would say Chinese faith in this phenomenon of unceasing effort is at a level most Americans cannot comprehend.

Indeed, if I had to impart something of the uniqueness of the Chinese spirit with one story, I would use "The Foolish Old Man Who Moved Mountains", for it represented a reality I witnessed every day: when I did my early morning runs and saw scores of undergraduates walking around campus reciting their lessons, each convinced that dogged perseverance was the key to his success; when my own students confided in me about their life dreams and the detailed plans to accomplish these; when I thought about the economic miracle that marks the China of the last twenty years. "The Foolish Old Man Who Moved Mountains" was the reason I was certain, despite reading stories to the contrary, that China would complete its Olympic preparations in time for the event.

Of course, belief that you can achieve the impossible through dogged perseverance alone has a dark side as well. Convinced that a gigantic increase in steel production was the key to turning China into a first-rate power, in 1958 Mao Zedong tasked the entire country with undertaking this project, essentially transforming every household into a home smelting operation. Known as the Great Leap Forward, this would turn into one of the greatest collective efforts humanity has ever engaged in, and one of the greatest failures. Not only were millions of acres of forests denuded to stoke the furnaces, but the subsequent redirection of labor resulted in unharvested crops and massive famine. To top things off, the steel that resulted from all this sacrifice and hardship was practically worthless.

Philosophy, it should be added here, is never far below the surface in any culture. For example, the ideology behind "The Foolish Old Man Who Moved Mountains" can be found in the *Tao Te Ching's* notion that the yielding element of water can wear away the hardest rock. Or again, the farmer discussed earlier who loses his horse but manages to keep his calm is firmly grounded in Taoism's claim that since reality is in a constant state of transition—hot becoming cold, the young turning into the old, those who are healthy developing sickness—it makes no sense to focus too long or too hard on one state of reality because it will soon transform itself. Just as one cannot hope to get a handle on America without at least a basic acquaintance with the Bible, so a familiarity with the classics of Chinese thought is similarly a prerequisite for getting beyond a surface understanding of the country and its people.

But back to our story: I closed my introduction to the topic of fate that evening by telling the group the Somerset Maugham parable known as "Appointment in Samara." A servant spots Death in a Baghdad marketplace. When Death seems to beckon him, the servant flees and asks his master for permission to leave for Samara in order to avoid Death. The master agrees. Later that day, Death stops by to visit the master and mentions that she was surprised to find the servant in the market in Baghdad, since they were scheduled to meet the next evening in Samara. The point, I concluded, is that you cannot avoid your fate. *Dui bu dui*? I asked. "True or false?"

"I do not think it is true. I believe I am in control of my life," said Lionel, who was certainly in control of many of the conversations. "It is like Forrest Gump says, 'Life is like a box of chocolates.'"

Before I could piece together the analogy, Marlene was already on the offensive. "That is not what the box of chocolates means," she shot back. "The chocolates are simply surprises in life. They are not fate."

"But you can do what you want with the surprises in your life," Lionel replied. "You do not have to be controlled by them."

"Of course that is correct," she said. "But the box of chocolates has nothing to do with fate."

The controversy was tossed into my lap. In truth, it seemed to me each side had a point, depending on which part of the analogy you emphasized. If you focused on the chocolates themselves, the meaning might be that just as we don't choose what's in the box, neither are we in control of the events of our lives. This would give the image rather fatalistic overtones. On the other hand, one could point out that since it is up to us to decide what to do with the chocolates—we can eat them smilingly, spit them out, or simply throw away the box—the analogy is more correctly viewed as tilting toward validating freedom of will. Maybe this "two sides to every coin" thing was rubbing off on me. Of course, it was always possible, to paraphrase Sigmund Freud, that sometimes a box of chocolates is just a box of chocolates. In any case, for the purposes of the present discussion, it was a distinction without a difference.

"Regardless of how we interpret the box of chocolates," I said, "it seems the two of you are in agreement that we are in control of our lives. Is that correct?"

"Yes," said Lionel.

"Of course," echoed Marlene.

"What about everyone else?"

A young man who I had not seen before spoke: "My father was a poor farmer," he began. It seemed as if he had much more to say and was formulating how to say it in a second language, and then, deciding the effort was too great, simply added, "And now look at me." This led to a discussion of farmers who had become entrepreneurs, of girls from humble origins who had worked their way to the top and, of course, of the Chinese equivalent of *American Idol*, the *Super Boy* and *Super Girl* contests. All these examples were offered as demonstrative proof of the mobility of Chinese society, unshakable evidence that even those furthest down the economic ladder could, through dogged perseverance, make it to the top. The American Dream, I remember thinking.

My mind flashed to a large billboard in Chunxi Lu, the major shopping area in Chengdu. A shoe company that shall remain nameless had depicted an American basketball player I didn't recognize in the midst of an impressive slam dunk. Underneath the picture was the slogan, "Impossible is Nothing." At first, I thought this might have been a mistranslation, since bad renderings of Chinese into English are more the norm than the exception here. But a quick check of the original Chinese written besides it verified that the wording was indeed accurate. Both the English and the Chinese were a play on the more common "nothing is impossible," expressing, if possible, an even more hopeful sentiment than the original.

It was an ideology I had heard echoed numerous times in one of my writing classes. There, I had given the students an assignment loosely based on National Public Radio's *This I Believe* series. Originally airing in the fifties and recently revived, the show consists of famous and not-so-famous people reading five-minute summaries of their philosophies of life. I tasked my class with composing similarly styled essays expressing their own worldviews. Since the radio essays invariably began with the author completing the phrase "I believe" with some string of words that provided a concise summary of their personal credo, the first assignment for the writing class was to likewise create a one sentence statement of belief. More students than I care to remember handed in the statement "I believe impossible is nothing."

Fatalism expresses the exact opposite sentiment. For fatalism, everything is impossible, except that one set of events that is predetermined by whatever forces are in control of the universe. It was this attitude rather than the "I am the master of my destiny" philosophy that I had expected to find tonight. Perhaps I had been relying in part on an image of China that placed it in line with other ancient cultures, in particular Greece and India. Despite the rationalist bent that is sometimes ascribed to them, the Greeks had more than their share of superstitious beliefs, including the tenet that the day of one's death was woven into the fabric of one's destiny on the day of birth and that nothing could alter this verdict. The most famous Greek play, *Oedipus*, is a literary embodiment of fatalism. When it is foretold that their child will kill his father and marry his mother, Oedipus's parents engage in what essentially amounted to the Greek version of family planning and abandon the baby in the woods. Although the infant is rescued and raised far away from his birthplace by another family, in the end Oedipus unwittingly fulfills his horrible destiny. Ancient India, with its doctrine of caste and belief in reincarnation, offers an even stronger showcase for fate.

Indeed, I think it is fair to say that in ancient cultures a belief in the inevitable is more the norm than the exception, and that historically speaking China falls into this pattern. The earliest writings we have in China are known as oracle bones: questions etched on tortoise shells (sans the tortoise), shattered, and then used to predict the future. As Lin Yutang, one of the major interpreters of Chinese culture to Americans in the middle of the last century, put it in his book, *My Country and My People*,

> Fatalism is not only a Chinese mental habit, it is part of the conscious Confucian tradition. So closely related is this belief in fate connected with the Doctrine of Social Status, that we have such current phrases as "Keep your own states and resign yourself to heaven's will," and "Let heaven and fate have their way." Confucius, in relating his own spiritual progress, said that at fifty, he "knew heaven's will." At sixty, "nothing he heard could disturb him." This doctrine of fatalism is a great source of personal strength and contentment, and accounts for the placidity of Chinese souls. As no one has all the luck all the time, and as good luck apparently cannot come to all, one is willing to submit to this inequality as something perfectly natural.[1]

Writing at the start of the current century, Richard Nisbett had reached essentially the same conclusion: "Westerners are the protagonists of their autobiographical novels; Asians are merely cast members in movies touching on their existences."[2] The verdict seemed to be in. The self-determination that is so much a part of the Western psyche is simply not a trait of the Chinese mind.

The only problem was that no one had told the group gathered here tonight. And they were none too thrilled to be informed I had expected them to fit into some long-standing stereotype.

"This is old China," said Sophie, dismissing the Lin Yutang quote that I had just read in order to gauge the reaction of the room.

"Yes," added Carrie. "We believe that we can do whatever we want with our lives."

"Is that the general consensus?" I asked.

"Yes," said everyone.

I had to admit to being a bit stunned. I told them that they sounded exactly like my American students. For over a decade and a half I had taught what is known as the "free will problem" in my Introduction to Philosophy class. Of the thousands of students who had taken the course, I declared that I could not think of one of them who did not likewise believe she was not in complete control of her destiny. They were even less pleased to hear this than the Lin Yutang quote.

The next day, as usual, I tried out the topic on my tutor Li Jiang. Did she believe in fate?

She did. "We have a Chinese saying," she explained. "*Ming ming zhe zhong zi you zhu zai.*" Seeing the helpless look in my eyes, she went on to translate: "It essentially means that in the unperceivable progress of the world, there is a power that is in control of everything." Although I wasn't clear on the precise meaning of her words, it was obvious enough the sentiment expressed a belief in the notion of fate. When I informed her of the outcome of the previous night's discussion—that not one person in the group expressed an affinity for this point of view—she seemed a bit distressed but not surprised. The attitude of young people toward fate, she replied, was just one example of how they were losing touch with traditional Chinese culture.

I would go one step further and offer an explanation of why this is so— take it for what it's worth. Although China is technically engaged in "socialism with Chinese characteristics," this differs from capitalism in ways the untrained observer would be hard pressed to discern. On this point, I am reminded of nothing so much as a comment from an old radical history professor of mine. "Communism," he would say, "is the oppression of man by man. With capital- ism, it's the other way around." While an almost religious belief in the virtue of economic progress is certainly understandable given China's past, one could see how it would wreak havoc on a conception of fate. Whereas a belief in fate is more likely to encourage acceptance of one's lot in life, a country's economic growth relies in large part on citizens becoming better educated, getting higher paying jobs, and buying more things than their parents.

Good riddance to fate, you might say, but I was not so sure. Ironically, the stresses of economic development might make a belief in fate all the more necessary. This is because economic competition will have winners and losers—usually more losers, in fact—and a doctrine of fate, as Lin Yutang points out, is one way to salve the wounds of winding up on the wrong side of this game. I was reminded of my counterpart teacher and Li Jiang's friend, Wang Jiali. Although they were about the same age, the two seemed to symbolize contrasting viewpoints on this issue. Despite having a good job at the university, Wang was eyeing an upwardly mobile lifestyle while Li Jiang seemed to have settled resignedly into her preordained path. Before I could ask her what she thought her friend's attitude on this topic might be, Li Jiang inquired, as she often did, about America.

"Do Americans believe in fate?" she asked.

Not really, I said, and went on to tell her about my American students.

"What about you?" she asked.

I was a little different. I let her know I was a big fan of the ancient Greek Stoics, who were actually quite sympathetic to the concept of fate. To prove my point, I reached over on my little bookshelf and grabbed a slender volume, one of the few books I had brought over with me from America—the Stoic classic, *The Handbook of Epictetus*. I read:

> Remember that you are an actor in a drama, of such a kind as the author pleases to make it. If short, of a short one; if long, of a long one. If it is his pleasure you should act a poor man, a cripple, a governor, or a private person, see that you act it naturally. For this is your business, to act well the character assigned you; to choose it is another's.

She was quiet for a long time. And then, just when I thought she was ready to resume the lesson, she let loose with about as high of praise as I ever heard from her regarding any Westerner, living or dead. "That man," she said suddenly, "is not far from wise."

EIGHT

What Is Sanity?

The discussion of fate was the last one of the school year, which meant I was halfway through my service. There were times, especially at the start, when I did not think I would make it even this far. I remember being so frustrated with one of my first oral English classes that I ended up not only walking out but also seriously contemplating an early return to the States. The group of students that brought me to this point was not officially part of the college; rather, as best as I was able to determine, their parents had either pulled some strings or forked over some serious cash in order to get their sub-par children admitted to a university.

I called them "sweathogs," a term taken from the seventies sitcom *Welcome Back, Kotter*. In that best-forgotten series, John Travolta played the leader of a group of lazy, wisecracking, though ultimately lovable remedial students who were taught by an alumnus of the high school, the eponymous Kotter. Unfortunately, my sweathogs possessed none of the charm of their namesakes. My counterpart teacher had them as well and so could sympathize. Much more diplomatic than I, she referred to them as "the difficult students." About the only way to get their attention, she informed me one day, was to threaten to report them to the administration. Although the use of intimidation went against my pedagogical beliefs, like the old line about never forgetting a face, in this case I was willing to make an exception.

At such times, I felt like Tooter Turtle, the hapless cartoon reptile who would ask his friend, Mr. Wizard the Lizard, to use his magic in order to transport him to some exotic land for a great adventure. Invariably, Tooter would find himself in hot water (metaphorically speaking) and would shout out, "Help me, Mr. Wizard." This would be the cue for the lizard to recite the incantation, "Drizzle, drazzle, druzzle, drome; time for zis one to come home." In a flash, Tooter would find himself back home receiving a lecture from Mr. Wizard about how it was best simply to be satisfied with your current situation. But he never learned. Neither did I, it seemed.

Fortunately, these were not my only students, nor did our time together last very long. When the university was about to undergo a review that fall, the class was mysteriously cancelled a few days before the accreditation team arrived. Although for the most part—that is, except for the sweathogs—I enjoyed my teaching assignment, the philosophy discussions were the highlight of my first year, since I was learning more about China there than anywhere else by far. However, I had not started the discussion group until the spring, and convened sessions only every other week. So, despite that fact that it would mean a lot more work—I prepared pretty heavily for these meetings, not only putting together an introduction but writing up a list of questions and sketching out possible lines of discussion—my plan for the final year was to meet weekly. Once classes started I sent out an e-mail notifying members of the new schedule and the first topic. Fitting for a middle-aged man embarking on his second year with the Peace Corps and still with little idea of what he was doing there, our initial session of the new school term was, "What is sanity?"

Coincidentally, I had shown *One Flew Over the Cuckoo's Nest* as part of the film series I had established on campus. Despite what you might think, my purpose in screening the film was not to persuade the students to draw some parallel between the insane asylum the main character is committed to and their own country, nor to open up a discussion about whether individual self-expression meets the same bleak fate in China as it does in the film. Such blatant political gestures were verboten in Peace Corps world, and not without reason. Peace Corps volunteers are teachers, not diplomats, and are sent as a goodwill gesture on behalf of the American government. Indeed, we are not even called Peace Corps in China because of the perception that this organization primarily aids undeveloped countries in need of a handout. Instead, in China the organization is known as the U.S.–China Friendship Volunteers. Regardless of how each of us felt about the Chinese government—and there were a variety of opinions— we all knew our purpose and acted accordingly.

What was our purpose? According to the Peace Corps mission statement, the first goal of the organization involves "helping the people of interested countries in meeting their need for trained men and women." I once had an angry ex-pat accost me at a Chengdu McDonalds concerning what he perceived as the ludicrousness of the U.S. government aiding the Chinese in learning English. Not only were we giving the Chinese a competitive advantage over us in the marketplace, but we were assisting them in stealing our state secrets as well. Look, I replied. There are about sixty volunteers a year sent over and 1.4 billion Chinese. I seriously doubt pulling the plug on Peace Corps China is going to impede China's effort at world domination. From what I know of the country (see "The Foolish Old Man Who Moved Mountains" story), if the Chinese are determined to learn English, the Chinese are going to learn English.

A second and more vital Peace Corps goal—at least in China, I would argue—is "helping to promote a better understanding of Americans on the part of the people served." Now one might legitimately wonder about the validity of this aspiration given the fact that there are already enough foreign English teachers in China to populate a small country. What is the point of the U.S. government paying to send a few score more over there every year? First, I'm pretty sure that the cost of the entire Peace Corps China program is slightly less than that of a military toilet seat. So even if the sole purpose of the mission consists in nothing more than a goodwill gesture on behalf on the U.S. government, well, one should not underestimate the importance of such small tokens among the Chinese. As such, it seems one of the best bangs for the buck we have going. But more important, it is precisely because of the number of foreign English teachers in China that the U.S. government needs to be footing the bill to send a few dozen more over there every year. In all honesty, the occupation does not attract the most well-balanced individuals, and in my experience many of the freelancers are not doing perceptions of the United States in China any favors. By contrast, to a person, the volunteers I knew were culturally sensitive individuals who served as sympathetic ambassadors for our country's values. To some extent, the small ripple effect of the Peace Corps China volunteers is needed to balance out the rest of the crazies teaching English there.

For the record, I felt very little repression myself. The philosophy group and the film series were allowed to operate without interference, though I know of at least one instance when we were investigated. It was also clear to me that if I stepped over the line in classroom discussion, I would hear about it. Every class had a monitor whose job was to report any inappropriate discussion by foreign teachers, and I had firsthand knowledge of at least one non–Peace Corps teacher who ran afoul of the university when he had initiated a discussion on Taiwan. To be fair, he was a nut case and that could have been part of the problem as well. So although I may have engaged in some self-censorship, about the worst restriction I can report is an inability to access Wikipedia for most of my time in China.

No, the reason I screened *Cuckoo's Nest* was not political but aesthetic: I wanted to illustrate to my Chinese students the concept of the antihero in American film. From Marlon Brando in *The Wild One* to Peter Fonda and Dennis Hopper in *Easy Rider* to Robert De Niro in *Taxi Driver* and Jack Nicholson in *Cuckoo's Nest*, there exists in American film a type of protagonist who is not the morally virtuous character we are used to cheering for but rather an outcast who defies society's norms and sometimes its laws. For reasons that are interesting to speculate about, we are not only not repulsed by such behavior but, given the right conditions, we even admire its perpetrators. As far as I could tell from my limited experience, no similar motif appears with any frequency in Chinese film. So I was curious about what my students would make of R.P. McMurphy. In retrospect (and only in retrospect) their reaction was predictable. Although they had little sympathy for the chaos-creating, authority-defying Jack Nicholson character, neither were they cheering on the authoritarian Nurse Ratched. The consensus, perhaps not surprisingly, was the very Chinese claim that both extremes were mistaken.

In my introduction tonight I talked primarily about the relation between art and insanity, suggesting that although sanity is ostensibly the goal in our society, artists, who are notoriously more insane than the rest of us, nevertheless make invaluable contributions to society. In fact, Plato, known better as the father of Western rationality, actually spoke favorably of insanity: "Madness is given by the gods to insure our greatest good fortune." Plato also viewed love as a type of madness. I thought the group, always interested in affairs of the heart, might take up that topic from this angle. In fact, we would end up talking very little about love or art tonight.

This would turn out to be one of the last times one of my favorite group participants would be able to attend. Having recently graduated from Sichuan

Normal, Richard was now teaching math at a prestigious Christian high school in town. A devout Christian, Richard had kept that fact under wraps for most of the discussions he attended. But not tonight. Instead, he started things off by inserting a reference to the Divine into his very first comment. In my introduction, I had mentioned the fact that the American Psychological Association no longer considered homosexuality a mental illness might be construed as evidence for the claim that standards of sanity can change.

Richard was incensed. "Truth cannot change because God cannot change and God is truth," he said. "So the standard of sanity cannot change."

A very Christian (and un-Chinese) assertion, I remember thinking. "But our understanding can change," I replied. "And perhaps as we change, we get closer to the truth."

"Yes, that is possible," he said, considering the implications of that statement.

Then the conversation took a turn toward the unexpected. What, he asked me, does the Bible say about homosexuality? I thought at first he was testing me, or was simply going to riff off my restatement of the Bible's condemnation of homosexuality to argue for the insanity of homosexuals. Apparently, however, Richard's Christian training did not include any instruction in the actual text of the Bible, for when I rattled off the standard quotes condemning homosexuality, he seemed sincerely puzzled. Contrary to what I had just told him, it was clear to him that homosexuals were born, not made; hence, they could not be insane. If they were, the goodness of God's whole creation would be called into question. Although I admired the consistency of his reasoning and agreed with the bulk of it, I was worried he might repeat his speculation to his employer and suddenly find himself with a lot of free time on his hands. So, despite the fact that it would cost me my most analytical participant—since if he were out of work, Richard could then attend our discussions—I let him in on the whole homosexuality-as-violation-of-nature line.

Probably on no other topic was I as surprised by the attitudes I found in China than on homosexuality. Before I touched down in Chengdu I had a strong sense that as a result of the one-child policy, there in all likelihood existed a cultural prejudice against the practice, since the logical consequence of same-sex coupling would be the end of the all-important family line. After I arrived, this intuition was bolstered by the discovery that on issues of sexual morality, my Sichuan Normal students seemed even more prudish than my Mormon undergraduates in America. All told, the stars seemed aligned against homosexuality finding any sort of sympathetic hearing in China. So I was more than a little taken aback then, when a values survey I did in my culture class showed that nearly two-thirds of the students thought homosexuals should have the right to marry or some legal equivalent. Nor was this class an aberration, for the question polled the same, semester after semester, for the duration of my time in China. Although I am at a loss for a complete explanation, anyone seeking evidence for the power of art would have been cheered to hear how many times the movie *Brokeback Mountain* (though usually called *Broken Back Mountain*) was mentioned by students in elaborating their position. But since the issue of whether homosexuals were insane did not directly speak to the question for the evening, I tried to connect the dots. "Many who classify homosexuality as a mental illness seem to argue that the standard of sanity ought to be based on the way most people in that society actually do behave. What do you think?"

Christians were persecuted in Rome, replied Richard. And they were in the minority. So just because your views are in the minority does not make you insane. He was not letting this Christian thing go.

"You seem to be saying that there is one standard of sanity regardless of what the society accepts," countered Sophie. "But different cultures obviously have different standards. It is ridiculous to think there is one standard." Most seemed to agree.

Although Richard was in the minority on this one, he was more than holding is own. "But there is a single standard for physical health," Richard responded. "Why should there not be a single standard for mental health?"

That was good, I remember thinking. Perhaps too good. No one offered a response, but neither did I think they were convinced.

"OK," I said, trying to get things going again. "Here's something else to consider. America seems to have a high incidence of depression. What do you think causes this?"

I knew they would jump at the chance to take pot shots at America, but I wasn't merely being mischievous. Perhaps inspired by Richard's analogy between the mind and the body, Angelina declared that just as Americans did not take care of their bodies and got fat, because they did not take care of their social relationships, they got depressed.

"Americans are always doing things by themselves," said Equal. "In China you have many people around you. So you do not get lonely or depressed."

"Family is more important to the Chinese," added Marlene.

"So you are saying there is one standard of psychological health and that it involves things like family and healthy social relationships." Most seemed to agree.

"Is there no depression in China?"

"Of course there is," said Equal. "But if we feel sad we go jogging, dancing, do some sports."

"Or talk to a friend," said Marlene.

"Pull yourselves up by your own bootstraps?"

No one had any idea what that meant. "Never mind," I said. "Here is a problem though. If the cause of depression is the American way of life, then the way to cure it would be to adopt many of the behavioral changes you suggest—to live more like the Chinese. However, there is good evidence that depression can be cured without any lifestyle changes, simply by taking a pill."

I was pretty sure that there was a fallacy here, but I felt at least it would be a useful one. Most, however, had no idea what I was talking about, though it wasn't, as with the previous expression, a language problem. The group had simply never heard of Prozac. Once explained, the notion that you could just take a pill for sadness struck them as misguided.

Marlene chimed in first on this point. Her mother had two friends who were both very ill with the same disease. One was a very optimistic and positive person, the other anxious and worried. Although they both had the same operation, the optimistic person recovered and is fine, while the pessimistic, anxious one continues to have trouble and a prognosis that is not good. "It is our attitude that matters," she confidently declared, "not some medicine."

I could see this was going to be a hard sell. "Are there many psychotherapists in China?" I asked.

Blank stares. Fortuitously, Sophie's stepmother was a psychological counselor, so she provided an explanation in Chinese.

"Very strange," said Equal. "This is what we have friends for."

This wasn't as much off the mark as I initially thought, for I later discovered that the most Sichuan Normal offered to students who reported symptoms of depression was peer counseling. Another sign of the embryonic state of psychotherapy in China was the fact that after the Sichuan earthquake, students with no more than a B.A. in psychology were sent out into the field to do work that we would expect carried out by licensed practitioners. At that moment I was thinking I should try to get a job with Pfizer or whoever it is that makes Prozac. Western antibiotics were ubiquitous, even though most people practiced Chinese medicine. Buddhist and Taoist temples flourished in an atheistic Communist Party. Since this was a pragmatic culture that would not let ideology get in the way of a good idea, I calculated it would not take long before antidepressants caught on, and I wanted to be in on the ground floor. Dollar signs flashed before my eyes until I realized that pirated Prozac would in fact dominate the market. Damn!

We seemed to have tapped out this vein, so I asked one of my prepared questions. "Who is the most sane, psychologically healthy person you know and why?" I thought the answer might provide some clues to their conception of sanity.

Someone mentioned a motivational speaker who went around to college campuses, lecturing students on the traits necessary to succeed in life. Another person said that it was people in the countryside whose lives were the sanest because they don't have the stress and worries of those in the city. Not so, came a reply. In fact, those who live such lives are always worrying about not having enough money. This sort of existence is hardly compatible with sanity.

"It is children under ten," said Ruth, a new girl who would turn out to consistently have some of the most interesting opinions.

"Why?" I naturally asked, since Aristotle had specifically denied that children could be happy.

"After ten, every age is fraught with anxiety. Teens are always worried about their peers and obsessed with the opposite sex. In your twenties and thirties you are constantly stressed about your job and raising a family. By the time you reach forty you begin to look back over your life and think about all you have not accomplished. When you turn fifty, you have to start thinking about your health."

Speaking of Prozac, I was getting pretty depressed just listening to this.

"What about children in Africa or in a war zone? They are not happy," countered someone.

"Of course not," she replied. "I did not say all children were happy. I only said that if anyone was happy, it was children under ten."

No one disagreed.

NINE

What Is a Good Education?

Breaking with tradition, I assigned an article for the discussion tonight: "What is a good education?" Of course, I knew no one would read it. This was one of the ways in which my Chinese students were similar to their American counterparts. In other ways, though, their lives could not have been more different. And there were times, despite the fact that I was ostensibly performing the same job I had done in the States—teaching at a university—that it seemed like I had gone through the looking glass.

To begin, the Chinese undergraduate's life is structured in a way that is unimaginable to the average American university student. Unlike at an American university where one forms an ever-widening circle of acquaintances, the social life of the average Chinese college student centers on a small, tightly integrated group that shares living arrangements and course schedules, among other things. These class collectives, which tend to be relatively stable, are the main organizing unit of the students' academic and social life over the course of their college career. As a result, a Chinese student at a large university has little social contact with those who enter the institution simultaneously, even less with those who begin at other times.

For example, let's say the new freshman class of English majors numbers about two hundred. They will be split into six or seven classes of twenty-five to thirty, with each small group soon forming a Crazy Glue–type bond. Over the course of the next four years these two dozen or so students will not only take many of the same classes in the same classrooms, but they will also live together, eight to a room, in the same dorm. Cliques and hierarchies, as well as oddballs and geniuses, will emerge as they share sorrows and joys, food and drink, sickness and health. Think high school on steroids. The living conditions during this period would seem as alien to the American undergraduate as the social arrangement. As mentioned, students live six or eight to a dorm room containing minimal facilities. Showers are placed in a different building. Although the rooms have neither heat nor air conditioning, students are not allowed personal heaters or electric blankets in winters, or fans in the summer. Drinking water is not available in the dorms; rather, students must go to another building and fill up the ubiquitous large thermoses one sees all over campus. Finally, undergraduates must be in their rooms by eleven on weeknights and twelve on weekends, at which time power is shut off. The Spartans no doubt would have found it a spartan existence. Nor were these conditions unique to Sichuan Normal, since from everything I was able to determine, a roughly similar situation prevailed on the other volunteers' campuses. But few things impressed me more in China than the spirit in which these students, believing they were building a better future for themselves, their parents and their country, endured conditions that would have sent their American counterparts into hysterics.

At times, this collectivism could bring about some rather surreal results. During my first year our school underwent what in the West we would call the accreditation process. For weeks before an evaluation team was due to arrive, I had to alter the course of my early morning runs because the combination soccer field and track where I regularly worked out was filled with bleary-eyed students who had been hauled out of bed in order to participate in the a.m. exercises. Instead of the usual silence and darkness, my pathetically slow trotting was accompanied by the glow from overhead lights and a chorus of more than a thousand students counting in unison "one, two, three" ("*yi, er, san*") while being led in calisthenics by a man with a large bullhorn who looked none too happy to be there himself. It reminded me of nothing so much as the jumping jacks and toe touches the nuns would have us perform in grade school, while the tune of "Give that chicken fat back to the chicken and don't be chicken again" played on a portable record player. Even the graduate students, I learned from my tutor, were forced to participate. Thankfully, the disruption ended as soon as the evaluators decamped, although I was never able to determine what this early morning display of physical prowess had to do with academic accreditation.

The organization of college life, of course, is a matter of neither happenstance nor whimsy. I doubt anything in China is. As Richard Nisbett points out,

> In general, East Asians are supposed to be less concerned with personal goals or self-aggrandizement than are Westerners. Group goals are more often the concerns. Maintaining harmonious social relations is likely to take precedence over achieving personal success . . . For Asians, feeling good about themselves is likely to be tied to the sense that they are in harmony with the wishes of the groups to which they belong and are meeting the group's expectations.[1]

One can see this cultural mandate at work in the design of college life.

Back to the reading for the evening. In a short, two-page article from a recent *Newsweek*, the philosopher Martha Nussbaum had argued for the importance of a liberal arts education. First, she declared that because it brings students in touch with issues of gender, race, and ethnicity, a liberal arts education fosters sympathy with those who are different. In an increasingly interconnected world, this is of ever-increasing importance. Moreover, by focusing on competing points of view across time and among cultures, a liberal arts education also encourages the acceptance of diversity that is essential to a democratic way of life. By contrast, the current model of education, leaning heavily on science, math, and technology, fails for the most part to develop any of these capacities, leaving both society and the student intellectually impoverished. What did they think?

Perhaps it was the line about democracy, which to be honest when I assigned the article I hadn't noticed, but the group wasn't persuaded. If science and math are seen as more important than a liberal arts education in America—and if they aren't, then I've been teaching in some other country for the past fifteen years—the situation is exacerbated in China. Although one would have thought that this group, composed mostly of language majors, might be somewhat sympathetic toward a liberal arts education, they were for the most part willing to concede pride of place to math and science. The gist of their argument was that since China was still a developing nation, science and technology must take precedence.

Of course, they added, there was something to what Nussbaum had said. As I have pointed out, in China there is always something to be said for the competing point of view. In this case, that "something" was that it is essential in the world today to learn how to live with those different from us. With over fifty-five recognized minorities, totaling 10 percent of the population, existing harmoniously within the larger society, China was a model on this point, or so I was told. By contrast, since minorities in the United States were sadly oppressed, perhaps a liberal arts education was a good idea for Americans. This was not the place to have that argument, I decided, and moved on.

"OK," I said, trying to bring the discussion back to the topic, "so is the answer to the question that a good education is the Chinese model of education?"

This was a trick question. To admit the Chinese education system was superior to the American was bad form, at least with an American in the room. So I knew this would get some response.

"No," said Lionel. "There are many problems in the Chinese education system."

"Such as?"

Angelina broke the prolonged silence. "Many of us are bored by our studies. I do not even go to many of my classes."

Part of the problem lies in the fact that there is almost no incentive for the typical student at a Chinese university to excel at his or her studies. While the move from high school to college is made on the basis of a single exam (more on that later), the transition from college to the "real world" relies not on one's transcripts but mainly on the *guanxi* or connections that one has managed to accumulate. So while it takes a lot of effort to gain entrance to a Chinese university—at least to the better ones—it is almost impossible to flunk out of one. I was given a lesson in this academic fact of life early on in my time in at Sichuan Normal.

With only a few days left before the end my first semester, I was told that I had to prepare three separate final exams (along with the answers) for my culture class: one for the students who took the final, one for the students who failed the final, and one for the students who delayed taking the final for some reason. As long as I was on a roll, I thought, why not one for left-handed students and another for right-handed? In addition, I was informed that any students who failed my oral English class would have to be given individual make-up exams. Under these circumstances, there existed a natural incentive to write an exam that students would be able to pass. Regular faculty members, I soon discovered, had already cracked the code, and near the end of the semester would prepare and hand out review sheets for their students that essentially provided the content of the exams.

"What," I asked, "would a non-boring class look like?"

Angelina thought for a while. "It would be one that consisted of something besides memorization," she said sharply.

"Yes," said a new participant, a young man whom I had not seen before. "We Chinese are very talented at copying but not so good at creating." He rather embarrassingly admitted that China was recently forced to purchase some technology from Japan, which I gathered was something akin to the U.S. having to borrow money from France. This showed, he said, that China needed to develop a more innovative spirit. Perhaps this was something they could learn from America.

He wasn't just being polite. The lack of creativity in their educational system is a problem the Chinese government itself recognizes. Indeed, this very point was brought up by the president of Sichuan Normal in his prepared remarks at a banquet given for the Peace Corps director—and if it was in the prepared remarks, you could be pretty sure it was the party line. It was certainly the view of everyone I talked to who had thought seriously about the Chinese education system.

"The problem begins with the *gao kao*," said Sophie, who as usual had thought about an issue more than most. "We spend our whole high school career memorizing in preparation for this exam. How could we expect the model of education to change once we enter college?"

"What's the gao kao?" asked the newest member of our discussion group.

This was Richard who, for a while, was known as Richard the Elder, in deference to the converted Christian and recent SNU graduate who claimed the unadorned name for himself. Alas, work commitments had now made it impossible for just plain Richard to attend. The new Richard was a large man with a deep voice and a gentle manner—a former Catholic priest and retired American hospice worker who had come to China to study the language and learn the culture. After stumbling onto us via a search for Yahoo! groups, he had contacted me inquiring about the possibility of attending our discussion group. At first, I was a bit uncomfortable about letting another foreigner into the discussion. Too many Americans, or the wrong kind—one who was convinced that the American way was the one right way and felt compelled to inform every foreigner about this belief whenever the opportunity presented itself—would have threatened the level of openness and frankness that was beginning to develop. Fortunately, Richard turned out to be a perfect fit. Like me, he was more interested in hearing the students discuss their culture than in illuminating them about the virtues of the American way. Tonight, he was in for the first of many lessons in Chinese life.

"Who wants to start?" I began.

The silence was not surprising. Inquiring about the gao kao to this group was like asking people who had undergone root canal without anesthesia to describe their experience.

"It is the test that every Chinese high school student must take if he wants to go to college," offered Lionel.

"So is it like the SAT?" asked Richard.

No more than jogging for a lap around the track is like running a marathon, I replied. Whereas in America a variety of factors—SAT scores, high school grades, letters of recommendation, extracurricular activities—play a role in college admission, in China there is one and only one determiner of one's fate in this area: the gao kao. The equation was simple. Those with the high scores get into the better colleges, those who do about average attend the Sichuan Normals of China, and those at the bottom quickly learn the Chinese equivalent of "Would you like fries with that?" Since those from the best colleges get the best jobs, and since there is almost no chance to change colleges (or majors, for that matter) once your initial assignment is given, the time for social mobility is before college, not afterward. Knowing this, these students and their parents deal with incredible pressure when gao kao time rolls around, in the spring of their senior year in high school. To rework a line from the movie *The Usual Suspects*, although they may not believe in destiny, these students certainly believe in gao kao, which is the next best thing.

The tests had been put into place after the disruption of the Cultural Revolution, the period from 1966 to 1976 when everything that passed for normalcy in China ceased to be. Up was down, black was white, and most colleges were closed. The concept of a single test to determine one's future, however, has a long tradition in China. Imperial examinations based on the writings of Confucius were instituted in the Sui dynasty and lasted more than thirteen hundred years until the overthrow of the Qing Dynasty early in the last century. Currently, the gao kao takes place over two days and ranges over four areas: Chinese language, English, math, and a "student choice" section involving either a science track or a humanities track.

Richard was horrified. "What a crazy system," he said. Of course, that comment pretty much solidified support for the exam among group members.

"It is difficult, but it is fair," declared Lionel. "Everyone takes the same exam, so everyone has the same chance to get into the best university."

"How is it done in America?" Sophie asked.

Between us we explained the basic outline of the American college admission process. But no one was very impressed.

"If the system is so fair, how did George Bush get into Yale?" asked Marlene.

"You have a point there," said Richard. "But don't unqualified people get into the best Chinese universities?"

It may happen, but most thought it was a relatively rare phenomenon, and none of those in attendance tonight felt cheated. "But there is this problem," interrupted Lionel, uncomfortable with having been pushed into touting the virtue of the Chinese way over other systems. He went on to explain that those from rural areas have poor primary and secondary education systems and so naturally do worse on the exam. This was an inequality China was starting to address, but it would take time.

"Well, we have the same problem in America," said Richard. "Many minorities and those who grow up in poverty have dropout rates significantly higher than the rest of the population, and far fewer of these individuals go to college, much less to the best colleges."

For all their complaining, it turned out that the students felt about the gao kao the way many Americans feel about democracy: it is the worst system for deciding who gets into college except for all the other ones. Richard wasn't ready to overthrow the SATs, but he did see the theoretical virtue of the Chinese system.

More important, Richard had passed his own test. After his initially bumpy critical comment, he had emerged in the group's eyes as not the typical American who was going to jump down their throats. Rather, this was someone who would listen, and perhaps even learn a thing or two. It was, I think, the start of a beautiful friendship.

TEN

What Is Human Nature?

I was always hearing from students, colleagues, and friends how different the Chinese were from Americans. Although I believed there was merit in much of what they were saying, my philosophical nature inclined me to argue the opposite. As a result, my general reaction was to declare that since we all wanted the same things—a good job for ourselves, health for our family, and prosperity for our country—we were a lot less diverse than they believed. One of the first and most frequent replies I received in response to this assertion was that whereas those in the West believed that as a result of original sin humans are inherently evil, no such conception existed in China. Tonight, I would finally get to take a run at this topic.

I began my introduction by pointing out that the view in the West was not as monolithic as they might have been led to believe. To be sure, mainstream Christianity accepts the doctrine of original sin. And since the majority of Americans are Christian, the implications of this were far from culturally insignificant. But not everyone in America is Christian, I argued, nor does every Christian take this rather pessimistic attitude toward human nature. Moreover, the Western tradition contains other stances on this topic besides the standard Christian one. The French philosopher Jean Jacques Rousseau, for example, believed man to be inherently good but corrupted by society. By contrast, the British thinker Thomas Hobbes used empirical observation and not Christianity to conclude that humans are greedy bastards. Finally, I reminded them that one should not overestimate the extent to which the American people had cogitated on this issue. The truth was, frankly, that most of us were too busy watching *American Idol* to worry about questions regarding the ultimate essence of their being.

Before I could throw out the first question, however, Ruth had something she wanted to present. Ruth was a student of my new Peace Corps sitemate, Kristin. I felt fortunate that the Peace Corps had assigned Kristin to Sichuan Normal. Having recently graduated with a philosophy major, Kristin took an immediate interest in the group, bringing not only her enthusiasm but also a number of the graduate students she had been assigned to teach with her. Many would cycle in and out, but Ruth was one of the more steady and earnest participants. For tonight, she had put together a handout summarizing the basic views of human nature to be found in Chinese philosophy. According to Confucius (551–479 BC), men are neither good nor bad at birth but develop a character in one direction or another depending upon their environment. Mencius (385–303 BC), a follower of Confucius, believed humans to be essentially good and possessed of an inborn sense of compassion and morality. Finally, Xunzi (312–230 BC) took the view that although our human nature inclines us to do bad things, we can overcome this tendency through training and study.

People immediately began to take sides, and for a while the discussion alternated between those who thought humans were naturally good and those who believed they were morally neutral at birth. No one was laying claim to the position that man is inherently evil, leading me to suspect that the group had entered into a conspiracy of silence in order to prove the point about original sin being a Western idea. But then another thought suddenly occurred to me. Perhaps a vocabulary derived from the story of the Garden of Eden was not the best language in which to couch the discussion. I tried a different approach.

"What do you think about the idea that humans are naturally selfish?" I asked.

At this point Pioneer, the philosophy graduate student, jumped in to make a familiar point. "I do not think we are answering the question," he began. "The question for the evening is, 'What is human nature?' But we are asking instead whether human nature is good or bad, selfish or unselfish."

Although I shared his concern, I felt the focus on self-interest was appropriate in this instance. "True enough," I said. "But sometimes these related issues can help us uncover a definition. So I'm going to let it go."

"Of course people are selfish," uttered Marlene, more or less ignoring Pioneer's interruption. "If there is a piece of cake on the table, we would all want it for ourselves."

"Why else do we go to school," added Sophie, "except to get a good job for ourselves?"

"What about having children?" I asked.

"That is selfish too," replied Marlene. "We want someone to take care of us when we are older."

Either the terminological shift or Marlene's rhetorical abilities had definitely changed the attitude in the room. Most assented to the proposition that humans are selfish, except Pioneer, who still seemed to be nursing some resentment from having his suggestion rejected. "If someone falls down a well, I will feel pity," he said. "This shows there is a natural sympathy in humans." Later, I learned the example was lifted from Mencius, although the well should have tipped me off that the story was not exactly a modern one.

"How do you know what the person feels?" asked Marlene.

"How do you know he does not know what the person is feeling?" I interjected, lifting a line from my favorite Chinese philosopher, the fourth-century BC figure Chuang Tzu. Chuang Tzu is the next great figure in Taoism after Lao Tzu, though their respective works are as different as night and day. Whereas the *Tao Te Ching* is a tightly crafted work consisting of oracular verses that can come off sounding like they should be carved in stone, the book that bears Chuang Tzu's name is a series of rambling stories and vignettes, many of them quite humorous. My favorite story in the *Chuang Tzu* involves a monkey keeper who tells his charges he will give them three acorns in the morning and four in the evening, and when they get all upset he says, all right, I will give you four in the morning and three in the evening, which for some reason placates them. I think about this story every time there is an election in America: will the three-in-the-morning or the four-in-the-morning party win? Chuang Tzu allows you to look at the world and laugh—a necessary part of maintaining one's sanity. In the particular story I referred to in my reply to Marlene, Chuang Tzu is staring at a slow-flowing river and comments on the fish's happiness, whereupon his companion skeptically questions whether Chuang Tzu in fact knows that the fish are happy. "How do you know I don't know the fish are happy?" asks Chuang Tzu triumphantly.[1]

Since no one seemed to catch the reference I briefly recounted the story.

"There are many Chinese sayings about this," said Carrie, breaking a prolonged silence.

"About fish?" I asked.

"About human selfishness."

So much for the Chuang Tzu story. "For instance?"

"*Ren bu wei ji tian zhu di mie*," she began. "This means 'Heaven and earth will destroy those who don't think about themselves.' It implies that all the people are supposed to first look out for their own needs."

"This saying reminds me of another," added Marlene. "*Wu du fei zhang fu.* Its literal meaning is that 'Ruthlessness is the mark of a great man.'"

"There is also *ren wei cai si, niao wei shi wang*," responded Carrie, not willing to be outdone. "Translated word by word, it would read, 'People are willing to die for money just like birds are willing to die for food.'"

"I personally hate these absurd sayings," interrupted Lionel, who seemed a bit embarrassed by the direction the discussion was taking. "Actually, most Chinese people know the sayings, but we usually don't stop to think about the subtle connotations. I think it's an exaggeration to claim that everyone in the world is selfish and there's no exception."

"But do these sayings imply selfishness or self-interest?" I replied. Everyone seemed puzzled, understandably so, since it is a fine enough distinction to comprehend even if English is your first language. So I explained.

"A selfish act often advances our own good at the expense of another, while a self-interested act can simply be one that does me some good but concerns no one else. For example, it is selfish for me to eat a candy bar in front of a group of hungry people and not offer to share, whereas it is self-interested to tie my shoes so that I don't fall. It benefits me but doesn't harm anyone else."

"And sometimes an act can benefit me and someone else," added Ruth.

I thought she was just trying to illustrate once again the Chinese preference for compromise between two extremes. But more was at stake here. "Sure," I said. "What's your example?"

"*Guanxi*," she said.

"Of course, guanxi," I replied. The proverbial light bulb turned on over my head. How could we have gone so long tonight without mentioning guanxi?

"What's guanxi?" asked Richard, who was about to get his second Chinese lesson in as many sessions.

No one said anything, so I jumped in.

"The word literally means 'relationship' or 'connection,'" I began. "But that doesn't really help. The closest Western equivalent is the idea that, 'You scratch my back, I'll scratch yours.'"

"So what's the big deal?"

The big deal, I wanted to say, is that guanxi is the social equivalent of oxygen. Just like life would stop without oxygen, Chinese society would grind to a halt without guanxi. But I checked myself.

"It's not a big deal," I replied. "It's just something you have to be very cognizant of in China."

Indeed, as if it weren't difficult enough to learn Chinese, the Peace Corps pounded it into our heads during our ten-week training that we had as well to master the language of guanxi if we wished to flourish at our sites. It went something like this (and as they say, the following is drawn from real life): Suppose your academic supervisor asks you to help him with a translation. Although you could refuse, if it ever came to the point where you wanted something, say, a faster Internet connection, well, there might be a problem. Conversely, if someone does you a favor, even if they offered to do it without your asking, assume you will be expected to do something in return. Of course, no one would ever come out and say, "If you want your Internet fixed you will have to do the translation." That would be too crass. But neither was it left unmentioned. This is where that wonderful Chinese indirectness comes into play. The supervisor wouldn't say, "You did not help me with the translation, so you are not getting your Internet upgraded." But he wouldn't turn you down without somehow mentioning it, saying, for example, "Yes, I will do it as soon as I get this translation finished," or something to remind you of your unwillingness to assist him.

In addition, there were all sorts of unofficial rules about guanxi that circulated among the volunteers. My first sitemate, Spencer, for example, believed profoundly in the notion that there was a shelf life for guanxi with respect to foreigners. He reasoned that since the relationships in which most Chinese found themselves were relatively stable ones that they could count on continuing indefinitely, they tended to keep a long memory about such matters. But because the guanxi space in the brain was filled with these types of commitments, foreigners had to call in their favors within a relatively short period of time, otherwise the claim would be conveniently forgotten. I wasn't one hundred percent convinced about this one, but why risk it? But guanxi has a dark side as well. We lost one volunteer during the training period owing to a "guanxi gaffe," when he rudely returned a gift from a Communist Party official he had helped out.

I explained all of this to a wide-eyed Richard.

"So if someone does me a favor I should assume they are not doing it just to be nice."

"Well, you can look at it that way," I replied. "Or can focus on the fact that they are giving you the opportunity for you to do something for them, which is letting you into their guanxi circle."

"How does it work in America?" asked Lionel. I could feel a slap down was forthcoming, so I let Richard field the question.

"Well," Richard replied, "sometimes you do something just because it's a nice thing to do, not out of self-interest."

"But most Americans are Christians?"

"Yes."

"And Christians are rewarded in heaven for their good deeds?"

"Sure," said Richard, a little hesitantly. "I guess so."

"So then there is guanxi with God."

"Hah," said Richard, letting out a big belly laugh. "I guess that's right."

"But it is true," Lionel began to walk it back, "that we do not have the same spirit of charity and volunteering that exists in America. This is just starting to develop here." He went on to state that a large part of the explanation for this could be found in the fact that China's economic development was a recent phenomenon. "As Maslow said, before we can do higher things one must first have the basic needs met," he added apologetically.

I could vouch that many Chinese would express surprise when they discovered that I was serving as a volunteer for two years. Most thought I was somewhat retarded to do so, but there were always a few who applauded my effort, adding invariably that China in fact had similar programs which sent students into the Western regions of that nation.

"But if humans are essentially selfish," I said in response to Lionel's defense, "what's the motivation for engaging in charitable activity or volunteering?"

"I guess that might prove humans are not essentially selfish," he said.

I was waiting for someone to respond to this line of reasoning, since the fact that people engaged in volunteer activity hardly disproved the thesis of egoism.

Perhaps they had some selfish, ulterior motive? But the room went quiet, as it occasionally had a tendency to do. So I decided to change the subject. Recently on *Meet the Press* (which I was able to download once I got a faster Internet connection) I had heard the American evangelist Rick Warren discussing his rationale for trying to bring Christianity to China. Essentially, he had argued that just as Christianity had saved the United States from the excesses of capitalism, so China needed some moral scheme in order to check the unbridled greed that was spreading along with free market economics in the country. What, I asked the group, did they think of that?

"Maybe he should be preaching Christianity in America," said Lionel. "There seems to be no shortage of greed there."

"Yes," added Carrie. "There is a story we tell. The American president asks the people what they want, and they say, 'More.'"

Richard laughed. "You have a point there."

"We do not need outside help in order to behave well," Pioneer added scornfully. "Confucius provides us with all the motivation we require to act morally."

"It's interesting that you bring up Confucius," I said. "He seems to be making quite a comeback these days."

"You mean Yu Dan," said Lionel.

"Precisely," I replied. One of the most popular figures on the contemporary literary scene was a professor whose books had attempted to demonstrate how ancient philosophers like Chuang Tzu and Confucius were still relevant to contemporary Chinese society. Yu Dan, a forty-something media communications scholar at Beijing Normal University, was not only allowing ancient philosophers to speak to the current generation; she was also becoming wildly successful in doing so. Her books and videos of her lectures were selling like, well, whatever the Chinese equivalent of hotcakes would be.

I began to speculate on what the implications of Yu Dan's success might be on our topic for the evening. "One might," I argued, "see these works as filling a sort of value vacuum, thus implying that humans are naturally selfish and need these tendencies to be curbed. On this view, Confucianism would be playing the same role in Chinese society as Christianity does in Rick Warren's America."

Everyone was quiet.

"On the other hand," I said, more or less thinking out loud, "if humans were naturally evil, they would hardly be seeking out Yu Dan's books, which offer a level of moral guidance. So perhaps her success indicates a basic goodness in humans."

"As we say," said Lionel, "there are two sides to every coin."

"Actually there might be three here," I began, "since we still haven't mentioned the possibility of humans being neither good nor evil. But since you brought it up, I would like to know finally what the heck this phrase means."

"There are two sides to every coin?"

"Yes," I said. "I have been hearing this almost since the moment I arrived in China, and I still don't understand it. And what I *do* understand just seems to be wrong. For example, are there two sides to how you interpret the phrase?"

"Well," said Lionel, "this is a long story."

"Perhaps we could take it up next week. Hint, hint," replied Kristin, who like me was intrigued by this phrase and was itching to discuss it at one of these sessions.

"Right," I said, understanding her meaning. "Since we are almost out of time, how about we decide right now the topic for next week will be, 'Are there two sides to every coin?'"

And so I would hopefully have one long-standing question about China answered. Or not.

ELEVEN

Are There Two Sides to Every Coin?

This was a moment I had long been waiting for, which probably says more about my life in China than about the topic. What was I doing here anyway? Did I want to see the world from a different perspective for a while? Was I going to change my life? Or did I just need a break? At some point, I would have to answer this. But for now I was satisfied waking up every morning knowing I was certainly not in Kansas, er, Utah anymore. Although much of my time was spent preparing and teaching a heavy course load—not unlike back in Utah—I also devoted a good amount of energy to studying the language, discovering the city, eating new foods, and developing a seemingly endless variety of intestinal problems. But learning about the worldview of my students from these weekly philosophical discussions was definitely the highlight of my experience. At least you didn't get tapeworm from new ideas.

I had been hearing the phrase, "There are two sides to every coin" almost from the moment I started teaching in China. In fact, I can recall my initial experience with the expression of this sentiment. As part of our training that first summer in China, we were required to engage in a stint of practice teaching at a local university. In preparation for the class, I had constructed elaborate lesson plans utilizing some of the more interesting philosophical problems I had lectured on in my previous life. One topic that transferred well to an oral English class was the issue of moral dilemmas—difficult situations that require a choice between two or more resolutions to a complex ethical situation. Part of the reason this exercise was so successful involved the Chinese undergraduates' predilection to perform. Although Chinese students are notoriously passive in the classroom compared to their Western counterparts, when given a chance to shine—be it in acting, speechmaking, or singing (especially singing)—they usually milk it for all its worth. If I did not understand this phenomenon, I nevertheless made the most of it, routinely requiring students to act out a skit at the end of whatever exercise I had assigned to them.

The particular moral dilemma that served as my initiation into the ubiquitous phrase "There are two sides to every coin" involved a married woman who was spotted by an acquaintance obviously carrying on with another man. Should the friend say nothing, confront the adulterer, or notify the husband? While the majority of the group that had been given this ethical situation to ponder felt the unfaithful wife needed to be dissuaded from her current course of action, the skit they presented avoided such extremes as severing the friendship or informing the husband, opting instead for a mild reprimand. Afterward, I opened up the dilemma to the class. What did they think about the group's solution?

"Of course," began the first young woman who raised her hand, "there are two sides to every coin." She then went on to explain that although having an affair was obviously wrong, the woman doubtless had an explanation for her behavior. Perhaps the husband was neglecting her, or was much older, or maybe she was madly in love. In any case, we needed to hear her side of the story before making a final judgment. As a philosopher, I was perhaps more disturbed by the general sentiment than by its application in this instance, since the solution seemed to suggest a reasonable middle way between extremes. But if there are two sides to every coin, does that mean the Nazi side was ethically equivalent to that of their victims? Doubtless, it was a bit of a stretch to move from adultery to the Holocaust, but logically speaking I saw no way to avoid the implication. Nor was I given a reason in the numerous times afterward that the phrase came up in conversation to think that anyone using it could fail to be implicated in its ethically disturbing consequences.

Philosophically speaking, the consequences are known as relativism—the belief that there exists no absolute right or wrong in ethical matters. For a relativist, it is not wrong to kill a fetus, but neither is there anything moral in letting it live. For a relativist, it makes no sense to speak either of a right to life or a right to an abortion because, for the relativist, when it comes to abortion—or any ethical issue—there is no truth, only opinion. So what I wanted to discover tonight was whether the phrase "There are two sides to every coin" was intended to convey relativism, and if so, how did the students respond to the obvious objections?

To start the discussion off tonight, I tried to strike a Socratic stance of true puzzlement, which wasn't difficult because I was truly perplexed. What the heck did they mean by the phrase "There are two sides to every coin"?

The first respondent, a young woman I hadn't seen before, stated that she saw the "two sides" claim as implying only that all events had a negative side and a positive side in the same way that a coin has two sides. She mentioned a Chinese phrase, "*you shi you de*," which she declared meant that in any situation you both give something and you get something.

Thoreau had said, "You never gain but that you lose something." Was this the meaning?

"Yes," she said, after someone explained it to her in Chinese, "I think it is something like that."

Another newcomer—we had been getting many since Sophie assumed the role of publicist for the discussion group and began advertising it on numerous websites and chat rooms—added that she understood the phrase as applying to persons. Although someone might be generous, she declared, they may have a dark side as well.

"Are you referring to anyone in particular?" I said jokingly.

"No," she firmly responded, seemingly concerned that she might have offended someone.

Finally Lionel jumped in, late for him. He had always interpreted the notion of "two sides to every coin" as involving the doctrine of the middle way. In every situation there exist two extremes, or two sides, and we should find the middle between these extremes. For example, one can sleep too much or too little. The middle way tells us to find the proper balance. At this point, someone—I don't remember who—held up the well-known yin and yang symbol. "There is a balance, and if you go too far to one side, there will be something that will come back at you." Although I wasn't sure which of the interpretations this was supposed to support, neither did I ask, in part because I was frustrated no one had mentioned any of the ethical implications of the phrase.

Taking matters into my own hands I asked, "What about 9/11? Is it the case that there are two sides, the side of the victims and the side of the terrorists?"

Understandably, no one really wanted to confront me on this one, so I straight out asked Angelina. "Yes," she replied. "Someone might say that the terrorists had a reason for how they acted."

"But was it a good reason?"

"Well, the proverb does not say there are two *good* sides to every coin."

Fair enough, I thought, and did not press the issue any further. Besides, I was trying to find out whether these students believed it was possible to make an absolute judgment about a morally heinous situation. If they did not, then I could feel fairly confident in labeling them relativists. But in order to find this out, I would have to present a situation that *they* truly found ethically horrible, and not one that appeared so to me. So I brought up the old standby.

"What about the Rape of Nanking?" I asked, referring to the slaughter of tens of thousands of Chinese by Japanese troops during World War II. The group had discussed this atrocity earlier when we attempted to define what was a hero. "Were there two sides to that?" It was a situation guaranteed to elicit universal contempt. Moral argument requires such scenarios as a baseline for discussion. For whatever reason, the murder of six million Jews during the Holocaust did not evoke the level of disgust in China that it did in America. In all honesty, at least among my students, Bush's failings were greater than Hitler's. So the Rape of Nanking it was.

"The people who did it obviously had a reason," said Lionel.

"But was it wrong?"

"According to us, yes," replied Lionel.

"But according to the Japanese?"

"Well, now even they admit it was wrong."

"But at the time?"

"At the time, they obviously thought what they were doing was right."

"And you and all other Chinese action judged the action immoral?"

"Yes."

"So how do we decide who to believe?"

"That," he said after a notable pause, "is difficult to say."

Although Lionel's reluctance to engage in outright moral condemnation was not necessarily shared by the majority of participants that evening, it is consistent with the mainstream tradition of Chinese thought. The vocabulary of good and evil, right and wrong has metaphysical connotations foreign to both

Confucianism and Taoism. The notion of "good" as we use it in the West does not mean "good for me" or "good for my family" or even "good for my country." Rather, the idea is that good is good from a universal, not a partial, perspective. Similarly, when President Bush referred to "evildoers," he was speaking at least in his mind in universal terms. But the notion of a universal good and evil requires a realm beyond the physical, for without such a sphere of being, everything is simply good or bad from a human perspective. In the West, this metaphysical territory is provided first by Plato and later by Christianity (which, as Nietzsche pointed out, is essentially Platonism for the masses). The beauty of Chinese philosophy is that it never plants itself outside of this earthly realm and so does not develop a conceptual framework that encompasses a universal notion of good and evil. Tao, the central philosophical concept at the heart of Taoism, presents a fundamentally different perspective on reality than anything in the West. A metaphysical absolute like God provides a clear vantage point beyond this world—a God's eye view, as it were. The Tao is "content with low places people disdain." The metaphysical absolutes of the West (like God) are able to be understood by reason, but the Tao is a "mystery that cannot be told." God is associated with light, while the Tao "dwells in darkness." And while God is only good, the Tao "gives birth to both good and evil."[1]

"So, then," I said, summarizing, "it seems at least one meaning of the original phrase is that every event, even something as horrific as the Rape of Nanking, will always be viewed from multiple perspectives, as being good to some and bad to others."

"I don't see how anyone can say that," offered Richard. "I mean, some things simply have no good side to them. Like the end of the world."

"Funny you should mention that," I replied. "Do you know the book *The World Without Us*? It was a recent best selling book in America whose theme was precisely all of the good things that would happen for the planet should humans be eliminated."

"I see," said Richard, laughing. "Bad for us, great for the algae."

The mention of algae sent my mind to the ocean and this sparked a memory of one of my favorite Chuang Tzu stories, which suddenly seemed to be relevant. "Does anyone know the 'Frog in the Well' story from Chuang Tzu?"

After the usual period of silence, Pioneer, the philosophy graduate student, chimed in: "A frog is living in a well, happily believing himself to be lord of quite a grand empire. One day he meets the turtle of the Eastern Ocean, and the frog begins to brag about how great he has it. But then the turtle describes the vastness of the ocean, and the frog is stunned into silence."[2]

"And the point, unless I'm mistaken, is that once you have seen things from the wider perspective of the turtle, the natural response is to step back from it all—which is exactly the point of Taoism. The Taoist retreats from the society."

"Yes," said Pioneer.

"By contrast, for Confucius, we have an obligation and duty to contribute to society. That's why Confucius spent his life trying to get an appointment from the state, whereas Chuang Tzu refused political office when it was offered to him."

Since no one interrupted I kept going with this train of thought. "So, I have wondered for a long time, what exactly is the relation between these two sides of the Chinese spirit? How exactly, if at all, do Taoism and Confucianism fit together in your mind? Is one right and one wrong? Or what? Because to me they seem to be like oil and water—polar opposites. But I know a lot of people who admire both. So what's the deal here? Enlighten me on this one."

It was a lot to ask and I had to explain the problem a couple of times, but eventually they understood my request.

"I think," said Lionel, "that for most people, the Confucian method is their philosophy of life. But if you cannot succeed along this path, then you can adopt Taoism."

"I disagree," replied Sophie. "I believe they apply to our lives as a whole. As children we are Taoists. As adults, we follow Confucius. But once we retire we become Taoists again."

"I always thought that they were two sides of the same person," added Marlene. "Sometimes we are Taoists, and sometimes we act as Confucius told us. So maybe on holiday we become Taoists, but during the week we agree with Confucius."

My head was spinning. But I think I could finally see the outline of a response to the objection that relativism does not allow for the criticism of evil. The implication from the discussion of Confucianism and Taoism was that opposites are interconnected parts of a larger whole that require each other in some manner, either in the same society, individual, or lifetime. This attitude toward opposites is exactly what the *Tao Te Ching* expresses: "Being and non-being create each other/Difficult and easy support each other/Long and short define each other/High and low depend on each other."[3] But if evil is a necessary consequence of having good in the world, if one opposite by the very nature of its being brings about the existence of the other, then it makes no more sense to criticize evil than it does to condemn death or anything else that is inevitable and necessary. It is simply not, according to the Eastern perspective, a rational response to reality. Following this line of thinking does not mean a nation (or an individual for that matter) has to roll over in the face of threats to security. But it does imply that one responds in full recognition of the elasticity of such labels as "freedom fighter" or "terrorist." Indeed, Deng Xiaoping's famous statement that it does not matter whether the cat is black or white as long as it catches mice—generally taken to signal a moral equivalence between capitalism and communism for the purposes of advancing the Chinese economy—is of a piece with this rejection of the vocabulary of good and evil.

I have set out an East-West divide on the notion of truth, especially moral truth, by ascribing an absolutist notion to the West while asserting that the East adopts a perspectivist interpretation according to which there are multiple viewpoints that are equally valid. In fact, there is a less than absolutist strain in American thinking that reflects the ideology embodied in the "two sides" proverb. In his book *The Metaphysical Club*, Louis Menand discusses how the philosophical movement known as pragmatism developed in part as a response to the Civil War, which had resulted from the clash of two absolutist conceptions of reality, each convinced that it had God and truth on its side. By redefining truth as "what works," the pragmatists had hoped to avoid the sort of either/or thinking they felt had led the nation to disaster. The view has at best a tenuous foothold in the American intellectual landscape, as evidenced by the last U.S. president, who spoke incessantly in the absolutist notions of good and evil that the pragmatists had hoped to avoid and that the Chinese have been doing without for thousands of years. There are obvious criticisms of this more "pragmatic" way of thinking, since no more than relativism would it be able to condemn 9/11. But then again, it may be worth keeping in mind that the 9/11 bombers spoke in absolutist terms much more reminiscent of the last president than of either relativists or pragmatists.

TWELVE

Is Marriage Necessary?

ortunately I had the perfect icebreaker for tonight's topic, one that had already been tested in my oral English classes. I'm not exactly proud of the origin of this particular lesson, but occasionally I would walk into those classes less than completely prepared. Since the main point was to have students speak English, it was not that difficult to wing it, though for the most part I put together rather extensive lesson plans. As I was pondering what would be the subject of our conversation on one of those days I was less than fully ready, I picked up a copy of *China Daily*, China's main English language newspaper. A cartoon on the editorial page caught my eye.

It showed a woman who had obviously just graduated from college standing at the proverbial fork in the road: one path went straight to an eligible young bachelor waiting in front of an upscale house, the other led to an intricate maze at the end of which sat an empty desk. Which one would she choose? Since my class was over 90 percent females who would be graduating in a year, I suspected they might have some thoughts on the topic—at least enough to fill the hour and a half time slot. My plan was to have the class break into groups, discuss the dilemma, and then share their deliberations with the remainder of their peers.

Interestingly, that staple of Western pedagogy, group discussion, is almost unknown in China. Its absence seemed to be related to what was my number one complaint about teaching in China—students absolutely refusing to pay attention when one of their peers was speaking. I would argue that both these characteristic features of a Chinese classroom spring from a model of education that sees the student as an empty vessel into which knowledge from an all-knowing source is poured—a view that explains the one-way communication style of most Chinese university classrooms. Lecture style predominates, and student success depends on little more than the ability to repeat back what one is taught. Why discuss things with each other or listen to fellow students speak when it is the teacher who is in possession of all wisdom? Although there certainly exist American university classes where regurgitation is the preferred mode of inquiry, having spent a good amount of time in academia I feel confident in asserting that the Western classroom is a very different beast. Nor is this merely an accident of geography; rather, it results from a radically distinct conception of the educational process. In his masterpiece, *The Republic*, Plato, the founder of Western educational theory, explicitly rejects the notion of the student as empty vessel, and instead advocates for a process whereby the learner contributes as much if not more to his own education than the teacher. True, Plato may have come to regret this insight when his own pupil, Aristotle, rejected all of his teacher's doctrines. But both the emphasis on what we call student-centered learning, where students assist each other in the pedagogical process, as well as the freewheeling atmosphere of many classrooms (in which the student is not only allowed but encouraged to confront the teacher) owe their origin to this distinctly optimistic twenty-five-century-old image. Here, I am saying nothing more than what most in the Chinese educational system would admit, and that, as I've already pointed out, the president of Sichuan Normal University stated at a banquet with the Peace Corps National Director.

But back to the cartoon. Admittedly, in asking students whether they would choose marriage or work I was presenting them with a false dilemma, since one could obviously get married *and* go to work. I was hoping the students in the oral English class would overlook this little inconsistency and engage in a fruitful discussion. In fact, the results were interesting enough that I decided to keep this lesson plan for my remaining oral English classes that week. Here is a representative sample of female replies, which broke three to one in favor of heading into the workplace instead of getting married: "I want to enjoy a life of working and maybe not get married. It is too easy, there is no challenge. . . . I want to live independently. . . . I want my life to be colorful; hardship is more important. I want to develop confidence. Without marriage, you can still have family and friends. . . . Many women feel they have to get married because family will depend on them. I do not care. I will go my own route. . . . Although the path will be difficult, I will enjoy it. If I choose marriage, it will be easy, maybe too easy. . . . I want to show my ability, confront obstacles. This is only possible with a job. . . . It is necessary for a woman to have a career and to support herself. . . . With a job, I contribute to society and fulfill myself. . . . I will study for my dream. . . . Marriage is a war. . . . The divorce rate is too high. . . . I need to depend on myself. . . . If you depend on your husband, when you get divorced, how will you support yourself?"

And the other side of the coin: "Career and job are important, but my heart tells me marriage is the most important thing. . . . Family is the most important thing in China. . . . Marriage, along with friendship and relatives, are the three vital parts of people's lives. . . . Marriage is our purpose, not a job. The purpose of a job is to help you have a wonderful family."

Here, I thought, were a number of strong, independent women who wanted to rebel against cultural expectations. Despite the enormous pressures for them to get married and have children, they were intent on going their own way. I was cheering for them, but not ready to lay down any bets. In some ways, the path of the independent women is more available in China than in the United States. Unlike in the ERA-less America, equal rights for women are enshrined in the Chinese constitution. Adopted at the Fifth Session of the Seventh National People's Congress on April 3, 1992, the Second Article of the Law of the People's Republic of China on the Protection of the Rights and Interests of Women reads, "Women shall enjoy equal rights with men in all aspects of political, economic, cultural, social and family life." Interestingly, women do not change their last names when they marry here, theoretically making an independent identity easier to assume within marriage.

Historically, however, the Chinese record on women's rights is far from stellar (can you say "footbinding"?). I won't go into details, but anyone interested in the topic should start by reading *The Good Women of China* by Xinran. Xinran hosted the first radio call-in show for women in post–Cultural Revolution China, and the book details some of the thousands upon thousands of women's stories she heard during this time. I will quote Xinran and leave it at that:

The position of Chinese women has always been at the lowest level. They were classed as objects, as part of property, shared along with food, tools and weapons. Later, they were permitted to enter the men's world, but they could only exist at their feet—entirely reliant on the goodness or wicked-ness of men. . . . Chinese history is very long, but it has been a very short time since women have had the opportunity to become themselves and since men have started to get to know them.[1]

Back to the cartoon, again. Much to their credit, tonight's group was too smart to get trapped by the false dichotomy expressed in the drawing. When I asked which path they planned to take, the mostly female audience said they had every expectation of achieving a career and marriage. Given the one-child policy and ready availability of willing grandparents, this desire was probably a more realistic goal than in the United States. But it was not totally unproblematic, as Sophie pointed out: "We may all want to have a family and a career, but in truth this is very difficult to achieve."

"But many teachers do that," came the response from one of the young men present, a newcomer.

"I meant a career, not being a teacher," Sophie sighed.

This was an important distinction. Although all of my students were osten-sibly being trained as teachers and would soon be performing internships at local schools, very few of them actually wanted to enter the profession. Teaching in China at the level below the university is perceived as primarily a woman's job, with the concomitant low pay and low status that goes along with such work in many cultures. My sense was that this group felt they had worked too hard and had too many opportunities available to fall into this career ghetto, though most would do precisely that.

I had noticed the same attitude during our Peace Corps summer project, which involved instructing a mixed group of middle school teachers and under-graduate education majors in Western pedagogy. During the first class, I asked the teachers to speak about their profession, hoping they would provide a few words of encouragement and an inspirational story or two to those who would soon follow in their footsteps. What I got instead was the South African Truth Commission, as teacher after teacher seemed to compete with each other to paint the bleakest picture imaginable of their profession. The winner (if that's what you want to call him) was a man in his forties who related how his dream had always been to go into business. Despite having failed at one opportunity, he was ready to launch into another one if only his school would let him take a leave of absence. Unfortunately, they had no intention of doing so. Nor could he just quit, since he had a family to support. His time, he said with a strange combination of defiance and resignation, had run out. Whenever I hear the term "broken man," I can't help but think of this proud spirit. To complete this bizarro-world picture, none of the education majors in the class wanted to be teachers either. Having caught the capitalist spirit of the times, each admitted to bigger dreams than could be contained in a classroom.

"Well," began Lionel, offering Sophie an option besides living alone or following the path of a career, "there are also the dinks."

"Did you say dinks?" I asked.

"Yes. Double income, no kids."

"I know what it means," I said. "I'm just surprised the term made it over here. And what do you think of the dinks?"

"The lifestyle is becoming more and more popular with young people."

"As is living alone," added Sophie, who seemed intent on making a point.

"Which brings us around to the subject," I said, having failed at first to connect the cartoon with the evening's topic. "Is marriage necessary?"

"Yes," said a new young man, "for the sake of society we need to get married and have children."

Marlene jumped in, begging to differ and aching for a fight.

"Life is short. I know what I want to do with it. I do not have time to spend on someone else's priorities. To be sure, I do not want to be alone. But I have friends, relatives, and family. I wish to live on my own terms. If I want to read a book I will read a book and not have to do the dishes. If I want to travel, I will travel. I will go where I want to go and do what I want to do."

Before anyone could counter, Angelina spoke up. "I do not know if I would go that far. I would like to find someone to live with. But I will never get married."

"Why not?"

"Because I do not want to get divorced."

"Your parents aren't by any chance divorced, are they?"

"Why, ah, yes," she said. "How did you know?"

"Lucky guess."

Tracy, who had not showed up for a while, entered the fray as well. "I just do not want to have children."

"But can't you get married and not have children?"

"No," she said. "I do not think so. My husband would want children, so I will not marry."

A fourth girl chimed in shyly, saying only that she agreed with much of what the other three girls had said.

This was too much for the men in the room, who seemed ready to lead an armed insurrection. Given the male-female imbalance in China, they were already facing long odds in their quest for a wife, and these women were just making things worse. "I feel sad that there will be four Chinese men without brides," said one young man shaking his head. It was good to know guilt wasn't only a Catholic weapon of choice.

Even more ominous words came from a woman, a graduate student also named Sophie, who made dire predictions about what would happen when these headstrong girls became childless, single older women. As if on cue, Tracy reversed course and told the story of her aunt. A strong and independent woman, her mother's sister had been her idol when she was growing up. Now, alone and unmarried at forty, she seemed more an object of pity than of veneration.

In truth, I didn't like the way the conversation was going. Although for the most part, the women were acquiescing to the idea of marriage, they seemed to be doing so reluctantly and with a decided preference for their careers. The men weren't much better. To be sure, they were gung-ho on matrimony. But in their minds the main motivation for the union seemed to be perpetuation of the Chinese race. I just wasn't feeling a lot of love here, to say the least. I sat back, watched things play themselves out, and decided to try to balance things out a bit next week.

THIRTEEN

Is Romantic Love a Myth?

As I said, I wasn't happy with the way the last session had ended. Believing myself partly to blame for the tone of the discussion, I was determined to seek redemption tonight. There was historical precedent for this. In the *Phaedrus*, Socrates starts off with a speech in support of the thesis that an invidual should give himself to a suitor who does not love him, since such an individual would be more rational than a lover, and consequently treat one better. Immediately after completing the speech, however, he realizes he has spoken blasphemously and recants, offering in response one of the West's greatest paeans to the power and beauty of love. I felt I had to least try to follow in his footsteps by making the case for romantic love tonight after having contributed to the beating it took the week prior. Our topic, put forth by me for the reasons just cited and agreed upon unanimously, was: "Is romantic love a myth?"

In my introduction, I explained that the notion of romantic love arose in the West for the first time in the twelfth century with the stories told by wandering troubadours. Up until that point, marriage had mostly been about property: either acquiring that of the wife's family or producing heirs for one's own. To be sure, passion had been around as long as recorded history. The Greeks not only knew about it but personified it as a god. But no one back then thought of spending life with one's erotic partner. Indeed, the Greeks had different words to describe the feeling we associate with erotic passion (*eros*) and the sensation connected to commitment and fidelity (*philia*). The combination of passionate emotion and lifelong fidelity is a relatively recent phenomenon and, some would argue, not necessarily a realizable idea. What, I asked the group tonight, did they think: was romantic love an illusion, or was it the real deal?

Since my main goal was to repair the damage to its reputation that love seemed to have suffered last time, I would not have asked the question in the first place had I not, like a good lawyer, been fairly certain about the answer I would receive. One of my main reasons for optimism was the popularity of *Titanic*, which routinely ranked number one among my students' favorite movies, and not because of any fascination with the history of navigation. Another indicator came in the form of one of the most memorable sounds I encountered in China: the giant "ooohhhh" of disappointment that would fill the classroom whenever I would cut off a romantic film such as *Shakespeare in Love* or *My Fair Lady* before it was finished. The premature ending of no other type of film evoked a similarly passionate response. The evening's conversation only confirmed my long held impression of these students—and their teacher—as, for the most part, hopeless romantics.

One of the newer attendees, Ren Yuan, started us off. "In China, we have the idea of romantic love long before the West. For example, do you know the story of the butterfly lovers?"

Since I did not, she agreed to enlighten me on the tale that has been called the Chinese *Romeo and Juliet* and dates back to the Tang Dynasty (618-907 AD). Dressed as a man in order that she might pursue the profession of the scholar (can you say "*Yentl?*"), Zhu Yingtai meets and immediately falls in love with the handsome Liang Shanbo. Wishing to continue her education, Zhu does not reveal herself, and the two study together as best friends for three years, during which time Liang somehow fails to discern his comrade's secret. (You would think thirty-six months of "No thanks, I think I'll hold it" every time they hit a public toilet might have tipped him off). Visiting Zhu's home after having completed his studies, Liang learns Zhu's true identity and proposes marriage. Unfortunately, Zhu has been promised to someone else. Heartbroken, Liang dies. On the day of her wedding, Zhu visits the grave of Liang, which opens up as she throws herself in. The two emerge as butterflies, to be together for eternity.

"Now I see why you all like *Titanic*," I said.

"What do you mean?" replied Ren Yuan.

"Well, they're the same story, aren't they? Two lovers meant for each other but tragically kept apart by circumstances."

"But they get together at the end."

"Only after death," I replied. "That's what makes both of these stories trag-edies, like *Romeo and Juliet*."

"I do not believe in such love," said Ruth. "It is a charming idea, but it does not last. I look at my parents. What we need is something much more real."

"Ruth might have a point," I replied, unable to stop myself from playing devil's advocate to my own plan to argue on behalf of love tonight. "Some peo-ple say that the reason stories like *Romeo and Juliet* and *Titanic* are so compelling is that the lovers never get together. If they did, all the passion would eventually end. On their twenty-fifth anniversary, Romeo and Juliet would certainly not display the enthusiasm they did when they first met."

"That is not true," replied Ren Yuan. "I have seen an old couple walking in the park hand in hand. So it is possible."

I contemplated the value of informing them that they were both engaged in what was probably the favorite logical fallacy of the group. Called the "hasty generalization," it consists of taking one or two examples and drawing a sweep-ing yet unjustified conclusion. Ren Yuan's old couple and Ruth's parents each constituted one individual instance and in no way warranted the inferences that had been drawn from them. Although I had been a stickler about it at the begin-ning, they had grown as weary of my pointing it out as I had of hearing it, so I saved my breath for the most egregious cases. Since this was a twofer, however, I decided I would say something when someone new jumped in. "Is there roman-tic love when people are starving?"

Or maybe it was the second biggest logical gaffe, after the non sequiter, or the irrelevant claim. But before I could counter the statement and bring the conversation back to the original question, Lionel decided to follow up on the remark in his usual way. "According to Maslow, one must fulfill the lower needs for food before any of the higher needs. So he would say that there is not roman-tic love when you cannot eat."

Things were threatening to spiral out of control. "Let's get back to original question," I said. "We have one person who believes in romantic love and one person who is skeptical. What do the rest of you think?"

"I think these things are not important for us Chinese," said a new girl. "I want someone to take my hand and say, 'I care for you the rest of my life.'"

"Yes," added Angelina. "I have heard that one reason the divorce rate is so high in America is that people have unrealistic ideals about love. We Chinese are more practical."

In truth, she had probably heard that from me. But I suddenly realized I had more important things to concern myself with.

"Pioneer's not here," I said, looking around the room.

"No."

"I should have figured, because by now he would have reminded us that we need to define romantic love before we can say whether or not it is a myth. So I'll ask it for him: 'What is romantic love?'"

It took a while for someone to respond. "Romantic love is a special feeling," said Ren Yuan.

Not bad for a start. One thing that had improved over time was the quality of their answers to the "What is x?" question. (And, despite what the previous remarks might indicate, they had actually gotten better at avoiding fallacies as well.) This was an issue Socrates confronted in the already mentioned *Euthyphro*. When Socrates asks the title character, who has just claimed expertise on the subject, for a definition of holiness, Euthyphro says holiness is what he is doing now, prosecuting his father for the murder of a household servant. The problem for Euthyphro, besides perhaps having the first-ever recorded Oedipus complex (well, second after Oedipus), is that such specific examples are not very helpful in illuminating definitions, since definitions by their very nature require looking beyond the particular instance to the general rule involved. Nor is this error only of historical interest. Ask someone for a definition of terrorism and you are as likely as not to get "9/11," or some such specific example, as a reply. The group—at least those who had attended regularly—had advanced beyond such obvious logical missteps.

"What kind of feeling?" I asked.

"What Ruth said, a feeling to take care of someone for life."

"But isn't that the way you feel about a family member?"

"Yes, but romantic love is different."

"How so?"

She thought for a while and then said, "I see the other person and my heart beats faster." Overcoming the urge to say that in the Appalachians this might not be an adequate litmus test to distinguish familial from romantic affection, I continued to ask questions.

"Does romantic love have to last a lifetime?" Yes, or it is not romantic love.

"Can it be toward more than one person?" No, at least not at one time.

"Can it be toward member of the same sex?" A unanimous yes.

"Can you have romantic love without sex?"

"No," said Sophie. "That is part of it."

"Yes," replied Ruth, "as long as you have that feeling for that other person."

I thought of the time I had showed *Lady Chatterly's Lover* to my culture class. I had stopped the film at the point where Lord Chatterly, who has returned from the war paralyzed from the waist down, urges his wife to take a lover. I asked my class what she should do. A majority strongly opposed the idea of her taking a lover, and even those who thought she should divorce her husband believed Lady Chatterly would still have an obligation to take care of him afterward (in much the same way, it seemed to me, that the students felt they would ultimately have a duty to tend to their aging parents). I truly could not imagine any of my Western students posing this resolution.

In any case, I summed up our conclusions. Romantic love is or involves a special and unique feeling toward a single individual, a feeling that evokes a desire to care for and commit to another individual for a lifetime. Although we probably could have explored the nature of this special feeling in more detail, I felt that, from a practical point of view, it would not have aided understanding of the issue. Like the Supreme Court justice who said he could not define pornography but knew it when he saw it, we had gone as far as I wanted to go tonight in supplying a definition. It was time to get to the money question.

"Well," I said. "Is this thing real or not? I mean, is this something that can last a lifetime?" I went around the room and queried everyone. It was unanimous. Even Ruth, who had initially objected, recanted and said that yes, she believed in romantic love but did not think that she would find it.

She was crying.

FOURTEEN

What Is the Difference between Eastern and Western Thinking?

The genesis of this week's topic deserves relating. My counterpart teacher, Wang Jiali, and I had an ongoing discussion about the differences and similarities between Chinese and American students. Since she took the side that there were fundamental dissimilarities, as was my standard operating procedure I felt compelled to argue the opposite. Recently, I had lectured in one of her classes on American attitudes toward love and romance—a topic of inordinate interest among my Chinese undergraduates. As part of the class I had played a scene from *Friends*, a show that was oddly still popular in China. Although, in my estimation, few of the tortures of hell devised by Dante could compare with being forced to watch a *Friends* marathon, I had to admit that the show possessed some insight into American culture, as evidenced by its long-term popularity. For this reason, it sometimes served as a useful pedagogical tool.

In the clip I played for the class, Phoebe was lamenting that her date had ended the evening with the words, "We'll have to do this again some time," which everyone except Rachel understood as the kiss of death. The scene continued by having members of the gang explain to Rachel how various phrases uttered in the context of romantic relationships meant the exact of opposite of their overt sense: "It's not you, it's me" means "It is you." "I think we should see other people" stands for "I already am." And, according to Chandler, uttering "I hope we can stay friends" amounts to saying "I am going to be dating leather-wearing alcoholics and crying to you about it." We actually had an interesting discussion on this last point, since it turned out there is a Chinese phrase that means girls like bad boys (*nan ren bu huai, nu ren bu ai*: literally, "Man not bad, girl not love"). Afterward, I had used this quote as further evidence to Jiali that there were more similarities than differences between our cultures.

To thank me for taking over the class, Jiali presented me with a book by Lin Yutang, an author I had not heard of at the time, but who, Jiali informed me, would help me to understand "the personality and characteristics of China and its people." Since I am already in possession of a reading list I will never be able to finish, I usually hate it when people give me books. But gift giving is serious business in China, and you express gratitude early and often. I was given a firsthand introduction into the solemnity of this practice early on in my time in China, when I presented the couple whose apartment I lived in during our training period with a bottle of wine as a token of appreciation. Despite the fact that neither of them drank, the father forced himself every night to have a half glass with me at dinner until it was finished. I reasoned now that if he could choke down the wine, I could speed-read my way through a book, regardless of my other obligations. As I started into the reading one evening, two things became apparent. First, the book was not merely offered as a gift (few things over here are what they appear to be), but was meant to further Jaili's side of the argument. Second, I would not be going to bed anytime soon.

Lin Yutang was born in southeastern China's Fujian province in 1895. The son of a Christian minister, Lin was educated at St. John's University in Shanghai. After receiving his degree, he taught for three years in Beijing before studying in America and ultimately receiving a doctorate in philology from Leipzig University in Germany in 1923. Moving to Shanghai in 1927, he began a prolific writing career that included founding several literary magazines. In 1935 he completed the book that would make him famous, *My Country and My People*. He would move to America in 1936 and continue to serve as a guide to the Chinese mind for Westerners. After his death the *New York Times* wrote that "Lin Yutang had no peer as an interpreter to Western minds of the customs, aspirations, fears, and thought of his people."

In the book, Lin discusses what he sees as the uniqueness of the Chinese character and the Chinese mind. Lin sums up the Chinese character with one word: "mellowness." This, he admits, is a quality "suggestive of calm and passive strength rather than of youthful vigor and romance." Rather than try to impose its will through action, the Chinese mind gives up on the world, and "flays its own hopes and desires." Far from leading to despair, this state of mind "enables man to find peace under any circumstance." Among the traits he sees as most characteristic of the Chinese mind are patience, indifference, pacifism, and contentment.

Patience is the result of the fact that "the Chinese people have put up with more tyranny, anarchy, and misrule than any Western people will ever put up with, and seem to have regarded them as part of the laws of nature." According to Lin, life instructs us to endure rather than to act. Although the willingness to suffer silently can result in a general indifference toward social injustice, this apathy to the prevailing social situation is an attitude "made necessary by the absence of legal protection," and will only be cured by constitutional protection for people's civil rights. In addition, Lin sees the Chinese as pacifistic, drawn to this position not because of idealism but as a result of common sense: "If this earthly life is all the life we can have, we must try to live in peace if we want to live happily." Although the Chinese man may desire many things, if he does not get them, according to Lin, he will happily settle for what he has. He wants some old, tall trees in his neighborhood, but if he cannot have them, a date tree in his yard will give him just as much happiness. He longs for a secluded hut among the mountains, but a caged bird, a few potted flowers, and the moon will suffice.[1]

Although this relaxed and essentially passive Chinese social attitude stood in opposition to the bustling energy of the America of that time, Lin believed that an even greater contrast existed between the Western and Chinese minds. Comparing the Chinese mind to a woman's (anyone looking for political correctness should look elsewhere), Lin declared that "the Chinese head, like the feminine head, is full of common sense. It is shy of abstract terms, like women's speech." Instead of analysis and proof, the Chinese intellect relies on "intuition for solving all nature's mysteries." This is why the Chinese mind "cannot develop a scientific method; for the scientific method, besides being analytical, always involves an amount of stupid drudgery, while the Chinese believe in flashes of common sense and insight." Hence, it is no surprise that logic never took hold in China, since according to the Chinese, truth "can never be proved; it can only be suggested." And whereas for a Westerner "it is usually sufficient for a proposition to be logically sound . . . for a Chinese it must at the same time accord with human nature."[2]

Such was the worldview I presented to the group at the start of discussion, without, however, ascribing a source to the position. What did they think? Did this accurately represent the distinction between the Eastern and Western mind?

"It sounds pretty racist," said Richard, the American hospice worker. "Why not just throw in 'opium smoking'?"

"I think this is the way people in the West used to view China," added Lionel, trying to strike a less truculent tone. "Maybe some still do. But I do not think it is accurate."

"You don't think that it is a very flattering picture?" I asked.

"No. I agree with Richard on that."

"Well, before you get too mad at me, you should know who wrote this."

"Who?"

"Lin Yutang."

"Did you say Lin Yutang?" As often happened, even when I thought I said a name or word perfectly, it would get repeated back to let me know I hadn't.

"Yes, the great Chinese writer."

"That was a long time ago," added Sophie.

"Well," I said, "there are only three options. Lin misunderstood the Chinese character so that his depiction is not valid. Or Lin's portrait of China was accurate for its time, but things have changed since writing it. Or Lin's portrayal was accurate then and is accurate today. Which one is it?"

The quickly reached consensus was that Lin was old school. In truth, I had expected a little more discussion on this topic. I was disappointed, because this description of the Chinese character presented a refreshing alternative to the constant busyness and restlessness of Americans.

"But that restlessness has created a lot of economic growth," said Lionel in reply to my lament. "This is what China needs right now."

"So it is a glorious thing to be wealthy."

"That is what Deng Xiaoping said."

"And do you agree?"

"Insofar as individual wealth makes the nation strong, yes."

"Is there anyone here who does not want to be rich?"

No one raised a hand. "And you're all doing this for the team, right?" No one seemed to understand my meaning, which was just as well.

"But there may be something in the claim that China is unable to produce science," interjected Angelina. "Look at how China is not really good at creating things. We are much better at copying."

"What's wrong with piracy?" I shot back, again playing the devil's advocate. "I mean, why not let others do all the heavy lifting and then merely copy their effort? Isn't that the smart thing to do?"

That struck a chord of recognition. I pulled out my copy of Lin Yutang and started reading. In the chapter on the Chinese character, he had described a type known as "the old rogue." This, he declared, was a Chinese ideal that had no real parallel in the West. "An old rogue is a man who has seen a lot of life, and who is materialistic, nonchalant and skeptical of progress," wrote Lin. The old rogue is shrewd, a little bit cynical and, like a good Taoist, takes the route of least resistance. As the name suggests, the old rogue outlasts and outsmarts those who may have a seeming advantage over him." Was this what China was doing by engaging in massive piracy, merely playing the old rogue?

"No, this is not right," replied Lionel. "Piracy is wrong. China must create its own products if it is to be strong."

"I don't know about that. It's pretty strong right now despite what many see as a lack of creativity. But are you saying piracy is wrong, or that it's not good for China?"

"Well, it can be both."

Not according to my writing class. In the argumentative writing course I taught that fall, I had taken on the topic of pirated DVDs, offering the class an example of an essay I had written on the subject as a concrete example of persuasive argument that they could then use as a model for writing their own essays. One of the boons, as well as one of the dangers, involved in teaching in China was the ubiquity of these incredibly cheap and technically illegal products. For about the equivalent of eighty cents you could own any movie you desired. Multi-season TV shows were available for a correspondingly inexpensive rate, with (to give you a sense of the going price) all nine seasons of *Seinfeld* costing about five dollars. Of course the quality of the discs varied wildly, and it wasn't like you got a money-back guarantee. Still, it was easy to get sucked into wasting time on this activity.

However, the main consumers of pirated DVDs were not foreigners but the Chinese public, especially college students, for whom the discs provided not

only cheap entertainment but a language-learning opportunity. Before presenting my demonstration argument to the class, I polled them on their attitudes and
found, unremarkably, that no one saw anything wrong about purchasing these
copycat films. I felt ready to pounce and put forward the following argument:

1. Any act that violates Confucius's claim, to not do unto others what you
    would not want them to do to you, is wrong.
2. Piracy violates this claim.
3. Therefore, piracy is wrong.

Generally speaking, there was no problem in getting the class to accept the
first premise, since Confucius's name still pulled a lot of weight. Indeed, as I've
pointed out earlier, the study of Confucius is back in vogue these days. In order
to make the much more difficult case for the second premise, I invoked an event
that was near and dear to all of their hearts: the upcoming Olympics.

"You all know," I began, "that China has paid a lot of money for the rights
to the Olympics, and one way they make this back is by selling merchandise associated with the Games. Imagine that people in America started selling pirated
Olympic gear at an incredibly cheap price, thus depriving China of money that
is rightfully theirs. Would that be wrong?"

"Of course," came the reply.

"OK. But when you buy pirated DVDs, aren't you doing exactly the same
thing, taking away income from those who have the rights to a product? If you
would not want Americans to deprive Chinese of income by purchasing pirated
Olympic merchandise, then it seems you should not cheat Americans who own
the rights to movies of income that is rightfully theirs by buying pirated DVDs."

Logically speaking, I had an airtight case—one that convinced precisely no
one. Americans, it was argued, make so much money that they can afford to buy
the real gear, while the Chinese, especially students, simply lack the funds to pay
the going price for legal DVDs. No effort was made to attack the argument itself,
which the class admitted was sound. At the time, I was frustrated, a feeling that
only lifted when I ran across Lin Yutang's words: "For a Chinese it is not sufficient that a proposition be logically correct, it must be at the same time in accord
with human nature."[3] Interestingly, Nisbett has some evidence to support this
supposition. In one experiment, Easterners were much more likely than Westerners

to fail to apply a universally sound rule to a particular example on account of the circumstance. Specifically, a rule to fire employees was acknowledged as sound by both groups but was much more readily put aside by Easterners when confronted with a sympathetic case. As Nisbett says, "To insist on the same rules for every case can seem at best obtuse and rigid to the Easterner and at worst cruel." My students would seem to concur.

While I was doing this exercise for the students, the *China Daily* ran an editorial on this topic. Although the writer argued against piracy, he failed to raise any moral or legal objection to the practice. Instead, he opined that by allowing piracy, China was becoming an embarrassment among the global community. By that time, I understood that saving face was much more effective as an argumentative tool than all the logic in the world—a fact that those discussing this issue, or any other Chinese matter, with the appropriate representatives might do well to keep in mind.

FIFTEEN

What Is the Value of the Past?

This topic requires some background information. My first winter in China I came across the following story in the online edition of *The New Republic*:

> There are 1.3 billion people in China. So how many Christians are there? 20 million, divided between 15 million Protestants and 5 million Catholics. Oh yes, how many celebrants of Christmas? Apparently, zillions, or maybe even more. So much so that ten goody-goody students, all at Chinese elite universities, have—according to BBC News—condemned the "rise in Christmas revelry...the proliferation of Christmas trees, seasonal messages and people celebrating 'until very late' on Christmas Eve." The critics exhorted the Chinese people to "resist Western cultural invasion." "This is a phenomenon of the collective loss of sense," said the critics. Who is to blame? asked the students. The government! So go back to Mao? No, not on your life. Go back to Confucianism.[1]

From the tone of the article, one would have suspected that *The New Republic* had uncovered some pocket of group hysteria infiltrating an otherwise sane nation, whereas for me, things appeared just the opposite. It sometimes seemed crazy for an entire nation to live without queuing in line, using credit cards, or drinking potable water. But I not only found the students' reaction to Christmas a rational response, I shared it. Indeed, to me the scene in Chengdu as Christmas approached was surreal. Nearly unrecognizable versions of *Jingle Bells*, *Frosty the Snowman*, and *God Rest Ye Merry Gentlemen* blared from the shopping malls. Carrefour, a large department/grocery store of French origin, featured a display of decorated Christmas trees alongside a wall overflowing with various seasonal paraphernalia, while at McDonald's the employees all donned Santa hats. Even the numerous mom-and-pop shops that lined the streets would throw in a string of lights or a picture of *Shengdan laoren* ("Christmas old man," i.e., Santa Claus), something to capture the spirit of the season. To complete the picture, the foreign teachers' residence at Sichuan Normal had been done up by our own Fred Mertz, Li Shifu (*shifu* being an honorific term for any workman), with a display that hearkened back more to Halloween than Christmas. Dozens of cardboard Santa Claus faces, still wrapped in the original plastic, hung from the branches of the trees, which gave the appearance of nothing so much as Old St. Nick being lynched—and which may well have been what Li had in mind, since my sense was that he did not much appreciate this assignment. In Chengdu, the whole process culminated on Christmas Eve, with masses of young Chinese going to the central shopping district and hitting each other with inflatable bats—a scene that was repeated in similar ways in towns across China (and that would be outlawed during my second year of teaching).

In America, of course, this enthusiasm for Christmas would have been unremarkable. But in China it just seemed, well, wrong. After all, these are the folks who put the "godless" in godless communism. To see the defining holiday of a Christian nation utilized as a walking advertisement for conspicuous consumption in such a land was disturbing—at least to me. Although I have nothing against Christianity, I also like a little variety in the world. Besides, a culture's holidays are not just a set of dates picked at random in order to take time off; rather, they are invariably connected to a higher set of values that in many ways define the society in which they occur. Take the case of our own holidays. During Thanksgiving, we try to cultivate gratitude; at Christmas, despite ever-increasing commercialization, people put forth sincere efforts to connect the holiday to its original spiritual meaning; for the New Year, we make resolutions, even though we may break them shortly thereafter. The point is that a holiday is related to some larger spiritual meaning, be it gratitude, holiness, or rebirth. Memorial Day and the Fourth of July are also linked to a societal purpose, most notably patriotism, which is a value all societies both promulgate and honor. To think that a society can simply choose a random day to celebrate just for the sake of celebrating runs counter to a wisdom that insists on a purposeful selection of such events as crucial to national identity.

This is where the protesting college students and I were in agreement: importing the central holiday of a capitalist and Christian nation does not bode well for an avowedly socialist and demonstrably atheist country. Not only were various local and national media reporting on the event, but the *China Daily* ran a number of editorials on the topic. Without going overboard in support of the students, the tone was on balance favorable. Here is a sample: "A certain point is reached in the course of Western culture entering the mainland . . . a certain point is reached in Chinese forbearance toward the entry of Western civilization." At such a point "great strains are produced and the party on the receiving side will finally protest." The writer concluded, "What is important is that the connotations of civilization or culture underlying specific phenomena such as boycotting Christmas and moving Starbucks out of the Forbidden City have wide-reaching, profound social and political influence and should not be overlooked."[2] Another had declared that "the PhD students' move still merits our admiration, for they had the courage to buck the trend."[3] *The New Republic*, I thought, had failed to appreciate the degree to which the students' actions had addressed larger societal concerns and captured the imagination of at least a segment of the educated Chinese population.

Nor was this the first time a movement emanating from academia advocated on behalf of Confucianism against a competing value scheme invading the nation. Han Yu was a scholar and government official who had watched with trepidation as Buddhism, which had been introduced to China probably in the first century AD, grew in popularity. For Han Yu, Buddhism struck at the very core of Confucianism and hence at the heart of China. When in 819 the emperor was preparing to oversee a ceremony in commemoration of the finger bone of the Buddha being brought to China, Han Yu knew things had gone too far. He composed a letter, known as his *Memorial to Buddhism*, in which he pleaded with the emperor to reconsider. Buddhism, he argued, was the antithesis of the state philosophy of Confucianism. Whereas Confucianism emphasized the centrality of the family unit to proper social functioning, Buddhism saw the family as unimportant. Hadn't the Buddha abandoned his own wife and child in order to take up the life of a wandering ascetic? What kind of a role model was this? If Buddhism becomes acceptable, he argued, there was every reason to believe that the people would follow Buddha's example and begin "throwing away their clothes and scattering their money." Rather than worshipping this "unclean thing," the emperor should hand Buddha's finger bone over to his officials to "cast it into fire or water." The emperor was not amused, and as a result it was Han Yu who almost ended up being cast into fire or water. But it was Han Yu who got the last laugh, as dissenters often do, although not in his lifetime. Not only did the Buddhist monasteries lose their tax-exempt status shortly after Han Yu's death, but Buddhism itself fell out of favor and has never since reached its previous level of popularity and acceptance in the national consciousness.

Although I am not a competent enough historian to judge whether Buddhism posed the existential threat to Confucianism that Han Yu perceived, philosophically speaking he certainly had a point. Indeed, it is hard to imagine a philosophy more opposed to the family-oriented, ancestor-worshipping Confucian view than Buddhism. Because the Buddhist monk takes a vow of celibacy, he leaves no children; because he abandons his family home for the monastery, he is unable to care for his parents when they are older. I'm willing to give Han Yu the benefit of the doubt here, for the fundamental principle he risked his life over seems a sound one: a society cannot survive without adhering to a core set of values. If the values are under attack by a competing philosophy, then the society itself is threatened.

So with yet another holiday season approaching, now seemed like the perfect time to pose the question of the value of the past. Surely, I thought, this group would come out with guns blazing against this mindless salesmanship so clearly at odds with the avowed ideals of their nation. Surely they would support their fellow college students in Beijing against this value invasion by the West.

"It is just a celebration. We go downtown and have a party on Christmas Eve. That is all there is to it."

"No one thinks about the symbols or the images."

"The music is nice."

I was alone in my outrage, it seemed. It was not the first time, nor would it be the last, that I completely misread a cultural situation. Just when I thought I knew something about this place, events would demonstrate that I still had a lot to learn.

"Just because we celebrate one holiday, does not mean we think about the values associated with the holiday," explained Nathan, a recent arrival on our scene.

"Maybe you should," I said, and went on to explain my Han Yu theory.

"But the case of Han Yu, the emperor himself was showing sympathy with Buddhism," shot back Nathan. "Our leaders are not guilty of any similar attitudes toward American values."

"OK," I said, throwing up my hands in defeat and returning to the original question: "What is the value of the past?"

"Of the four great civilizations—China, India, Egypt, and Greece—only China survived continuously," offered Daisy. "What does that say?"

"What does it say?" I asked

"A building that lasts for a long time can only do so if it has a strong foundation. Values are a society's foundation. Hence, what our survival shows is the strength of those values."

"Yes," said Nathan. "We cannot see the future, so we have to go back to the past. We have five thousand years to learn from. For example, we study poems from the Tang Dynasty as children in order to learn values."

"Can you tell me any?"

"Sure," he said. He thought for a minute, recited it in Chinese, and then provided a translation: "Hoeing under the midday sun,/Sweat dripping in the tilled soil,/Do you know in a plate of rice,/Every grain is yielded by such toil?"

"This poem tells us to appreciate the labor of the farmer and to think about how the food on our plate is the result of much hard labor," said Nathan.

"Yes," added Daisy. "This is how we learn many traditional Chinese values, from not having casual sex to the need to care for one's parents. People may not be able to explain them, but they are written on their hearts."

"Well," I said, "I think this is one difference between our cultures. America is a place that notoriously burns its past in order to build its future."

"Yes. You leave the places you were born and head west, while we mostly live in our hometowns."

"But isn't that changing?" I asked. "Isn't China becoming more mobile, with workers from the countryside going to the city and students from Chengdu seeking opportunity in Shanghai?"

"Yes, but we have a saying. 'The leaves fall close to the trunk.' That is, when it is time, we will return home."

At this point Kristin, the other Peace Corps volunteer, decided to enter the conversation. She listed three points, reciting them from a piece of paper on which she had been madly scrawling. "First, I think people just memorize values and because it is just rote memorization it does not always end up in action. Second, when people do act, they often act without reflection on these values. Third, sometimes people follow traditional values out of fear and not out of any belief that the value is correct."

"This may be true," countered Lionel. "But are things any different in the West?"

Before Kristin could reply, I jumped in: "What does it matter why they accept these values so long as they are worthy ones?" In particular, I had in mind the obligation to the parent that is felt so much more profoundly here than in my own country. Even if this duty is imparted through rote memorization, I reasoned, the situation in the United States on this matter was so disgraceful that I would gladly have a society forgo a little reflection on values if it meant fewer grannies get socked away in nursing homes.

"But what if they are bad values that are getting passed along and people follow these mindlessly?" replied Kristin. "Isn't that a greater danger than having no values?"

The problem in playing devil's advocate is that you sometimes end up arguing against things you believe in passionately. As a philosopher, of course I didn't view the mindless transmission of a value scheme as a particularly notable cultural achievement. Wasn't this precisely what Socrates had spent his life trying to combat, the fact that his fellow Athenians could not explain their fundamental moral beliefs? But neither could I approve of the value vacuum that existed—with the exception of the religious right (and that was hardly a model to follow)—in my own country. Was there a middle way?

SIXTEEN

What Is Funny?

I t was the end of my next to last semester in China. We had covered a lot of ground so far in the numerous philosophical discussions, much of it pretty weighty. Aiming to end this semester on a light note, I decreed the last topic this term to be: "What is funny?" Although it might have been more philosophically appropriate to focus on the theoretical aspects of humor, I just needed a good laugh. As a result, I told everyone to turn up ready to tell a joke. Philosophy tomorrow, comedy tonight!

I had become acquainted with Chinese humor as a result of my British and American culture class, which I would routinely begin by summoning my less-than-adequate level of Chinese to tell a short joke that seemed especially representative of American culture: dumb blonde jokes, lawyer jokes, you-know-you're-a-redneck jokes. Over time, I discovered a number of parallels between Chinese and American humor. To be sure, there were no blondes over here and so no dumb blondes. But there was the *hua ping*, or "beautiful girl with an empty head." And while the redneck per se does not exist in China, the influx of people from the countryside moving to the big cities in order to find employment had resulted in a number of jokes having to do with the inappropriate behavior of displaced rustic characters.

Inspired by a contest on the website *Slate*, I decided to devote one of my class sessions to euphemisms in general, and in particular to the euphemisms in our respective cultures for describing a stupid or foolish person. *Slate* had offered up the following as examples—"not the brightest bulb in the pack," "not the sharpest knife in the drawer," and "his elevator doesn't go to the top floor"—and asked its readers to submit their own. Interestingly, the bulk of the ones provided by my students involved the notion of having something in one's head, including but not limited to "water in the head," "ping pong balls in the head," and having one's head kissed by a pig. My personal favorite, though, was: "His IQ card is out of credit."

I especially liked this last one because it struck me as the most culturally revealing. In America, we would probably say his IQ card is "maxed out" or "past its spending limit." Although this may sound essentially the same as the Chinese version, in fact the American image implies spending funds one does not have, while the Chinese phrase does not permit this interpretation. This is because in China credit cards as we know and (used to) love do not really exist. To a large degree, the economy is cash-based, even in cities like Beijing, a fact that can drive many travelers crazy. Instead of having the credit card company set an arbitrary spending limit, in China one must deposit funds on the card in order to use it for purchasing. When you've used up the money on the card you are "out of credit."

Indeed, the very idea of credit cards—the notion that one would spend money one did not have—horrified most of my students. This attitude seemed to me not merely the result of a culture of saving but indicative of a philosophical worldview that is profoundly different than the Western one. I would argue that the very idea of the credit card has a particularly American flavor to it, embodying an attitude of optimism. Since Americans are certain that the future will be better than the present, we feel comfortable spending money we don't have. By contrast, the Chinese idea, which finds its philosophical basis in Taoism, is that because reality is in a constant state of flux—the young become old, hot becomes cold, what is hard is broken down into what is soft—one should take no course of action that makes overly optimistic assumptions about the future. Say what you will about the wisdom of this attitude, but I can tell you this: no Chinese would have taken out a mortgage that he knew was going to balloon in a few years on the hope that he would be able to refinance at the time based on the increased value of the house.

Although we might have some of the same sorts of jokes and sayings, not everything humorous translated easily from one culture to another. Soon after I arrived I started a cultural film series. It is not that the students lacked opportunity to see American films. True, few major releases made it over here to the theaters, and movie ticket prices were incredibly expensive relative to the average income. But cheap or free American movies were widely available. In addition to the innumerable shops that sold pirated DVDs, my university had almost any American film you would want on its website, complete with Chinese subtitles. As a result, Chinese students saw a lot of American movies. The problem in my mind was that what they wound up watching not only did not contribute to their understanding of American culture but often gave them a distorted view of my homeland. My students were convinced, for example, that *American Pie* accurately represented the sexual mores of the majority of my fellow citizens. My hope was that the film series could go some way toward correcting misperceptions by focusing on the best American films and thus achieving one of the three main Peace Corps goals, that of "promoting a better understanding of Americans on the part of the peoples served."

Before the films I would generally give a brief talk in order to provide some context. On one of the comedy nights I, appropriately enough, lectured on the subject, "What is Funny?" I began by reviewing the three general philosophical theories about what constitutes humor: Incongruity Theory, which sees humor as a response to an incongruity—a term broadly used to include ambiguity, logical impossibility, irrelevance, and inappropriateness; Superiority Theory, according to which humor arises from a "sudden glory" felt when we recognize our supremacy over others; and Relief Theory, associated with Freud and viewing humor primarily as a way to release or save energy generated by repression.

My plan was to follow this admittedly boring theoretical description with a concrete example of something funny in order to discuss how each of the theories might account for the humor. So, after a few minutes of lecture, a large image of a man getting a pie in the face appeared on screen. Who doesn't find a pie in the face funny? Apparently my Chinese students. In retrospect, I guess I should have seen that in a country where loss of face is the greatest fear, literally losing your face in a pie would be more horrific than humorous.

Fittingly, we began the discussion group with someone telling a joke I did not immediately understand. It involved a man who announced the news his wife had died to the servants by telling them to make only one egg for breakfast. After some probing, I discovered that what was supposed to be humorous about this was the tension between husband and wife. I immediately let loose with the few Rodney Dangerfield one-liners on the same subject.

"I asked my wife, where do you want to go on our anniversary? She said, somewhere I've never been. I said, 'How about the kitchen?'"

The puzzled looks on their faces upon hearing these made it clear why Rodney never played Chengdu. The next joke invoked another common pattern: poking fun at a local or regional character trait. Just as Texans can laugh at their tendency to do things in an oversized manner, so the residents of Sichuan seemed to enjoy making light of one of their province's most well-known features. Unlike the frenetic pace that prevails in much of China, this western region is known for its laid-back attitude and is often referred to as the leisure capital of China. Its residents are especially notorious for their fondness of (some would call it addiction to) the game of mah-jongg. So, goes the joke, China announces that it will send two astronauts from Sichuan province into space. Asked to explain how they decided on precisely that number, officials declare that if they sent three the astronauts would spend all their time at *duodijiu* (a popular card game requiring three people), while if four astronauts were involved they would be playing mah-jongg all day long (since that is the number generally required to play).

But it is one thing for a culture to poke fun at itself and quite another when an outsider does it. This, at least, is the lesson of the panda joke. Even today, it seems to me incredible that I managed to offend so many people with this humorous anecdote (that has recently had its punch line used as the title of a popular grammar book). A panda walks into a restaurant and orders a big meal. When the waiter comes to give him the bill, the panda pulls out a gun and kills him. As he is leaving the restaurant, the panda is asked why he shot the waiter, and he tells his questioner to look it up in the dictionary. Sure enough, the definition declares the panda to be a mammal indigenous to Sichuan province that "eat, shoots and leaves." Can you say lead balloon? My sin, it seemed, was in supposedly implying that the panda was a violent creature, when in fact everyone knows the panda is cute and adorable. Even pointing out the fact that the panda's lack of opposable thumbs made it next to impossible for it to use firearms did not assuage the student's indignation at my offending China's national treasure. To compensate for any perceived insult, I wore a panda shirt to all my classes the following week.

If they did not find the panda joke humorous, I was simply baffled with the most popular joke that evening and one of the trendiest types of jokes among my Chinese students: the "cold" joke (*leng xiaohua*). A kid asks his mom if he has a big head. When she says that, yes, he does, he runs outside and flies away just like a balloon. A man looks like an onion and so he cries all the time. A young penguin asks his mother if he is really a penguin, and when she says yes, he says, "Then why do I feel so cold?"

It is hard to know what to say about these, but I certainly could agree with the person who said that the purpose of these jokes was not to make people laugh. "The first time you hear it," came the explanation, "you don't understand it. After reflection, however, you see the humor." It seemed, however, I only reached the initial stage of this process.

We finished the evening in the realm of the political, which is about the last territory I expected to find myself in when the night began. Indeed, the Peace Corps warned us to tread lightly in sensitive areas, for example, advising us to avoid discussing the three Ts: Tibet, Tiananmen, and Taiwan. Hence I was a little nervous when someone offered to tell a Mao Zedong joke. Although not the uncritically revered figure he was following his death more than three decades ago (the official line, which I heard more times than I care to count, was that Mao was "70 percent right"), Mao was still greatly admired and regularly turned up on my students' list of personal heroes. But as long as I wasn't the one telling the story, I figured it was OK. It seems that Mao was engaged in one of his many love affairs. This time, however, his closest advisors had gotten wind of the activity and were taking turns lasciviously viewing it through a nearby window. Suddenly a door opened. Mao walked in and immediately began excoriating the group, lamenting that only his closest adviser, Deng Xiaoping, was not a part of this shameless cadre. One of those caught pointed out that the only reason Deng (who stood barely five feet tall) was not present was that he had gone out to find a chair to stand on. The joke went over surprisingly well.

But humor, of course, has its limits. And the things you can't joke about say as much about a culture as the things you can. It was no surprise that it was Angelina who crossed that line of what is appropriate. She would risk offending me, the group, or anyone in order to say what was on her mind and would continue to do so right up until the end. Tonight her transgression came in the form of a story about a Russian nuclear plant being victimized by an animal sneaking through the fences and destroying vital material. Through numerous photos, the creature had been identified as a rabbit; however, Russia's security detail, as well as crack teams from around the world, had been unable to capture it. It seemed hopeless until the Chinese police were called in. Within hours, they claim to have captured the perpetrator. At a hastily called press conference they drag out a badly beaten bear who confesses to being a rabbit.

I laughed, but noticing the somber mood in the room switched gears and tried to explain that the joke could be told about many American police forces.

"This is not something to joke about," said a serious young man. "It will cause people to lose respect for the police."

"Well, if she told it about the Chicago police, would you find it funny?"

"Yes."

"Angelina, why don't you tell the joke again. Only this time, substitute Chicago police for Chinese police."

She consented, everyone laughed, and there was one semester left.

SEVENTEEN

What Are the Limits of Privacy?

I was surprised it hung on as long as it did. The Joyful Reading Time Café always seemed to be struggling to keep its head above water. Every time I passed by I thought of Monty Python's infamous cheese shop, which was uncluttered by its featured product. Just so, our philosophical home for more than a year seemed unburdened by customers whenever we weren't holding court. Although I would try to give the place as much of my business as possible, living on a Peace Corps stipend, there was only so much coffee I could afford. I should have realized that things were going downhill when the owner converted the first floor into a clothes shop. In any case, returning after the semester break I was not exactly surprised to be informed that our philosophical home for more than a year had been replaced by a mah-jongg gaming room. I consoled myself with the belief that our meetings were probably the reason it lasted as long as it did.

It was time to find a different location, and quickly, since we were scheduled to start up in a week. Once again it was Sophie to the rescue. She not only found a suitable place near campus but managed to negotiate the drink price. The Macchiato Café sat on the second floor of a shopping center adjacent to campus, although I'm not sure shopping center is quite the right word for this three-level, open-air structure. The first floor contained an ever-changing assortment of cheap restaurants and student shops. In front of these stores a variety of independent enterprises had sprung up—flower shops, fast food carts, pirated-DVD tables—all illegally squatting in front of the legitimate businesses while paying them a kickback. This latter fact only came to light when I strolled over for lunch one day and discovered these makeshift shops victims of a pre-Olympic sweep by the city of Chengdu to clean things up. Their absence gave the ground floor the sense of emptiness of an apartment that's just been ransacked. At about the same time, most of the city's pirated-DVD operations, which had inhabited the upper floors of legitimate downtown electronics stores, were forced to go underground. The second floor housed the more expensive restaurants that served Chinese treats such as *mapu dofu, kongpao jiding,* and hot pot (*huo guo*). This last dish, Sichuan's most famous, is actually more of a social experience than a meal, involving as it does a group of friends, a selection of meats and vegetables, and a pot of boiling oil loaded with Sichuan peppers. I don't exactly know how to describe the taste of this whole conglomeration except to say I am pretty sure this is what they serve in hell. The third floor had more restaurants and something that passed for a gym, although none of the cardio machines ever seemed to work. On the plus side, membership was cheap. Finally, each level had one thing in common: a bathroom costing about two or three cents a pop and tended diligently by the guys with what has to be one of the worst jobs in China.

Given its surroundings, the Macchiato Café seemed surprisingly upscale, possessing everything our previous location lacked: carpet, comfortable chairs, and customers. Prices were a little steep, but as I said, Sophie was able to negotiate more reasonable rates. One drawback was that the place consisted of only a single large room. Whereas we had had the entire upper floor of Joyful Reading Time Café to ourselves, we would now have to put on our show in front of others. This, it turned out, would not be entirely unproblematic.

The first topic for our new location was, as they say, ripped from the headlines. It involved a not very technically savvy Chinese film star/pop singer named Edison Chen, his predilection for putting nude photos of himself and his many lovers (some of them also celebrities) on his computer, and his failure to realize that it is probably not a good idea to leave said photos on the computer when you take it to get repaired. Soon after Edison picked up his PC from the shop, the photos began appearing on the Internet. It wasn't long before Chen's was the most queried name on Chinese search engines, and the whole country—including our little corner of it in Chengdu—was talking about the scandal. After initially claiming the pictures were not legitimate, Chen, confronted with evidence, admitted their veracity and announced he was taking indefinite leave from his career.[1] Apparently, the Chinese entertainment industry had never heard the phrase, "There is no bad publicity."

At the introductory get-together for the semester, students had overwhelmingly voted to discuss the Edison Chen situation. I briefly contemplated applying the two-thousand-year rule and invoking my veto. After all, "What do you think of the Edison Chen scandal?" seemed more of a tabloid headline than the topic for a philosophical discussion. But interfering with the group's wishes would only dampen enthusiasm and lessen turnout. Besides, I realized there were numerous philosophical issues contained in Edison's misfortunes, not the least of which were questions about the nature and limits of privacy.

As an indication of the intense emotions generated by the issue, the sign I regularly posted on the ground floor of the Foreign Language Building announcing the discussion mysteriously disappeared—the first time this had happened. But if the vandals were hoping to suppress attendance, it was too late. Word had gotten out and the night of the discussion saw the largest crowd to date turn out.

Rather than give a long-winded introduction, which I suspected they had gotten as tired of hearing as I had of writing, I started with a simple question. "How many of you think that releasing the photos was wrong?"

Everyone raised their hands.

"Why was it wrong?"

"Edison Chen was the victim," said a woman who I had not seen before. As might be expected with a handsome male pop star, the women were particularly protective of Edison.

"What about the women in the pictures?" I asked.

"Yes, they were the victims too."

"But you still haven't explained why it was wrong."

"It was wrong because they should not have done it," replied the same woman who answered the first question.

As fallacies go, I hadn't seen many circular arguments in the course of our discussions, so instead of reading her the logical riot act I simply replied, "That's not really an answer." I went on to explain that we needed to state a reason why it was wrong. "We might say, for example, it is wrong to kill someone because it is against the law. So was there any law violated in releasing the photos?"

"I am not sure," said Pioneer. "But there are many things that are wrong even though there is no law about them." In fact, nearly a year later someone would be convicted for "obtaining access to a computer with dishonest intent" and sentenced to eight months in prison.

"Sure. It might be wrong for me to take Sophie's drink because she has paid for it," I said, reaching over and grabbing it. "And if she paid for the drink, then she has a right to drink it. Is that how you see it? Edison had a right to the photos?"

"I think," said Lionel, "this is a particularly American way of understanding the situation, as involving a right."

"Yes," said Ruth. "Whenever someone falls down in a store in America, they sue the owner. In China, we would blame the person who falls down."

"So why not blame Edison for putting the pictures on the computer, or not taking them off when he got it repaired?"

"Of course," said Lionel after giving it some thought. "Edison is somewhat to blame for putting the pictures on his computer."

"And what about for sleeping with all those women?" I added. "Is Edison to blame for this as well?"

"That," replied Lionel, "is a different matter."

"I'm not so sure," I replied, trying once again to play my self-assigned role as devil's advocate. "If Edison did something wrong or blameworthy, then perhaps publicizing it would be justified. I mean, if he had slept with twelve-year-old girls, then we might say that the person who published the pictures did a good thing."

"But he did not sleep with twelve-year-old girls," replied Angelina.

"I realize that," I said. "But if the wrongdoing is serious enough, isn't it a good thing to inform the public about it? Suppose, for example, he had been selling heroin. That would be a good thing for the public to know about. Would you agree?"

"Yes," sighed Angelina. "But he did not sell heroin."

"Well, if he did nothing against the law, why is he being punished?"

"As Pioneer said, there are many things that are wrong that are not illegal."

"Yes," volunteered Ruth, "what he did—sleeping with all those women— was wrong. Sex is not just about desire. It is about love."

"We are not just animals," added a young man I hadn't seen before.

"I disagree," said Angelina. "There is nothing wrong in what Edison did. Sex is a natural activity."

"It depends," said Sophie. "I think it is different if the women were married."

"So," I asked, "how many think that what Edison did, sleeping with a lot of women, was wrong?" The tally ran about four to one Edison's extramarital sex was wrong. Who ever said that if God is dead everything is permitted?

"OK," I said. "If what Edison did was wrong, then perhaps the person or persons who publicized it did a good thing. Maybe they should have been included on the list of moral models." Everyone caught the reference. The Chinese government had earlier in the year chosen fifty-three citizens as "moral models." These included a scientist who helped stem the spread of SARS, an agriculturalist who had developed the first hybrid rice varieties, a young singer who had given financial aid to nearly two hundred students and donated his cornea which enabled six people to recover their sight before himself dying at age thirty-seven, and a migrant worker who had sacrificed his life to save two children from getting hit by a train. At the ceremony Li Changchun, a member of the Political Bureau of the Central Committee, had said, "The whole of society should practice the socialist sense of honor and disgrace in a bid to support the economic and social development with strong ideological and moral power."

I had mixed feelings about the whole idea of a moral model. After initially recoiling at the concept, I had become more and more intrigued. In America, moral education is for the most part left up to the family. To have the government interfere in this process is seen by those on the left as crossing the line between church and state and by those on the right as infringing on the liberty of the individual. By contrast, in Taliban Land, the state not only sets the moral code but punishes violations of it by law. Perhaps having the state encourage a moral code but not legally enforce it was a reasonable middle way. Or perhaps I had been in China too long. In any case, the thought of putting the perpetrator of the picture release on the list of moral models did not go over very big, though it took a while to work out the details.

"The moral models did not harm anyone with their action," offered Pioneer. "But the person who released the pictures harmed many people."

"That's not true," replied Lionel. "One of those on the list of moral models turned in his boss for corruption. The boss was certainly harmed, as was his family."

"But in that case the only person harmed was someone who had harmed others," added Marlene.

"But wasn't Edison harming these women by corrupting their virtue?" I asked.

"They certainly didn't look in the pictures like they were being harmed," offered Angelina.

I started to laugh and realized I couldn't go any further with a line of reasoning I did not accept. So if what Edison did was wrong but not a serious enough wrong to justify publication of the pictures, what did they think about the fact that Edison had in essence been forced to step away from his career for a while? Wasn't this a bit hypocritical, if he had not done anything seriously wrong?

"What would happen in America?" asked Lionel.

Kristin stepped in. "First, I don't think anyone would have even looked at the pictures in America. If it's not video, it's not going anywhere."

"That's probably true," Richard added. "We have very short attention spans."

"Besides," I continued, "when Hugh Grant got pulled over because of a hooker or Kobe Bryant was accused of rape, their careers continued as if nothing happened. So I think in America we tend draw a line between private lives and public careers. For the most part, we don't think celebrities have any responsibility to serve as role models with their private lives. As a result, many behave very badly. How do you see it?" I asked "Do celebrities have a responsibility to set an example for society?"

"Yes," replied Ruth. "Celebrities should serve as moral models."

Everyone agreed.

So it seemed, perhaps not surprisingly, that there was much less of a private sphere for entertainers in China. In addition, there was no confessional media program one entered into in order to be forgiven—no Chinese Oprah (yet)—perhaps because the notion of sin did not exist. I was reminded of the ancient Greeks, who likewise lacked the notion of sin and substituted for it the concept of error. Of course, Oedipus and all the tragic heroes were punished for their mistakes. Just so, Edison seemed to be having retribution meted out against him, although I was not sure what his tragic flaw was. Bad judgment?

I couldn't help as well but think about the notion of saving face, according to which it is not the reality of the situation but how it appears that matters. As long as Edison kept his photos to himself, everything was fine. His sin or error (or whatever you want to call it) was going public. But this meant that if a morality was being demonstrated in this instance, it was a superficial morality based on appearances. But isn't a superficial version of morality and accountability better than the current ethical free-for-all in America? Perhaps not. Torn between the rock of hypocrisy and the hard place of moral chaos, I decided it was time to vote on a topic for the following week.

EIGHTEEN

Is Prostitution Wrong?

Tonight Kristin led the discussion. Since the plan was for her to be in charge of the group next year, I felt it was time to give her some practice running the show. It's not like it was rocket science. Sure, it helped to ask the right questions. But the hardest part of the whole thing was making sure people stayed on topic and spoke in English.

For her inaugural session, she chose an issue that she hoped would create controversy and stir up some lively conversation: "Is prostitution wrong?" However, it was not a disinterested love of animated discussion that caused her to propose this as the focus for the evening. Since arriving at Sichuan Normal, she had been hearing rumors about female undergraduates at our university who supposedly were picked up by wealthy gentlemen outside of the south gate on Friday evenings and whisked away for the weekend to play the Chinese version of hide the salami, though since cured meats are not really big over here, I'm not sure what that would be. The urban legend was certainly helped along by the fact that we had a modeling school on our campus. Kristin's American sensibility wanted to see this activity as a form of female empowerment. Unable to get a clear read on the local attitude toward this practice, she decided the group provided the perfect opportunity to test out her intuitions.

In an amazing coincidence, two days after the group voted to approve Kristin's topic, the governor of New York, Eliot Spitzer, was charged with using an escort service. Although we both thought this would provide an added impetus to the discussion, at the start of the evening we discovered that no one had heard the news. It was not that we had some America-centric view of the world and assumed everyone to be aware of the goings-on from our homeland. But since most of the students attending the discussions were English majors, it was not unrealistic to assume that they were familiar with the major American headlines.

Although they generally fulfilled this expectation, one could never be certain what stories they would latch onto as significant. Often these involved what they perceived to be some peculiarly American vice that was absent from China. Articles about gun violence, for example, were popular. I still can recall the excitement with which several of my students ran up to tell me about the shootings at Virginia Tech. Indeed, it is not an exaggeration to say the Chinese students I taught viewed America as one big shooting gallery. As someone whose own campus in the States allows students and faculty to carry guns to campus, I am not sure they were far from wrong.

Another category of stories that students were familiar with involved instances where America could be seen as complicit in some nefarious activity of which the Chinese felt themselves accused. It was for this reason that students were cognizant of a number of American food poisoning cases, product recalls, and disease outbreaks. Since sexual indiscretion by an elected figure fit neither of these categories, it was not surprising that the Eliot Spitzer saga did not register with them. Indeed, if the international reaction to the Clinton scandal taught us anything, it should have been that the rest of the world has a hard time understanding America's obsession with the peccadilloes of its politicians.

In the best philosophical tradition, Kristin began the evening by boldly putting forth three arguments. First, she pointed out that China seems to be taking to capitalism with a particular relish, adopting institutions as diverse as a stock market and private property. There is even a Chinese version of eBay. With everything seemingly for sale, why not sell your body as well? Second, she argued that in many cases prostitution may be the only possible means to a good end. Suppose a student wants to go to college but cannot afford it. One way she could earn the money relatively quickly is through prostitution—certainly much more quickly than the fifty cents an hour she would get working at McDonalds. Finally, Kristin hypothesized that sexual exploration can be one way toward personal discovery.

I admired her philosophical spirit. Cognizant of the unpopularity of her position, she advocated for it anyway. This is what philosophers do, I remember thinking. We throw arguments at people like cold water in their faces and hope that those thus treated realize they needed the splash to wake them up. Failing that, we try to run away fast enough to protect our skin. This latter course was the one chosen by Aristotle. When suspicion fell on him shortly after the death of his old pupil Alexander the Great, contrary to the example of Socrates, who drank his hemlock like a good citizen, the peripatetic philosopher declared he would not allow Athens to sin twice against philosophy and left town.

The expected backlash began immediately. Pioneer, the graduate student in philosophy, took issue with Kristin's analogy between selling other things and selling your body. "Your body is not just an object like other objects in the world. It is not even like an animal body. It has consciousness and intelligence." He had a point there. It was a pretty weak analogy, perhaps intentionally so.

"In China," Daisy added, "there is a moral line that values relationships. This is Confucianism. If we begin to believe that prostitution is moral, this will harm a man's family, not to mention the woman's freedom."

Lionel summed up what was a common consensus: "Every culture has looked down upon prostitution. Maybe there is something to it. There may not be a good philosophical reason for this. But we need tradition."

A newcomer tonight put it much more bluntly. "The family will be destroyed," she said, "if we legalize prostitution or cease to look down upon it." I guess I wouldn't be showing *Night Shift* for movie night.

Indeed, there was not one dissenting voice, not even the usually reliable iconoclastic Angelina, who instead offered up the claim, "Your body is not yours but was given to you by your parents."

It looked like it might be time to put on our running shoes. Indeed, the notion of a right to do what you want with your body is one that failed to resonate either in my classes or in the discussion group. Every semester I would give my students a survey to compare Chinese and American attitudes toward a variety of social issues: abortion, capital punishment, gay marriage, euthanasia, and so on. Although a majority of the class unsurprisingly favored legal abortion, very rarely was this opinion couched in terms of the right of the woman to do what she wanted with her body. Instead, students would talk about overpopulation or a family not being able to afford the baby or, in the case of a young girl, about how a baby would ruin her future opportunities. In almost all cases, the decision to have an abortion was seen as a tragedy.

"But what," I interjected, "would Li Yinhe say?"

It seemed only a few in the room were familiar with the name of China's leading, perhaps only, sexologist. Born in 1952 and with a PhD from the University of Pittsburgh, Li argues that if an action is (1) private, (2) done between adults, and (3) consensual, then it should be left alone by the state. In this spirit, as a member of the Chinese People's Political Consultative Conference Li has three times submitted proposals for legalizing same sex marriages—a suggestion that has been about as successful as the plan for a national day of recognition for the Dalai Lama. She has also argued that non-monogamous relationships are fine so long as both couples agree to the situation. And although she does not approve of prostitution and thinks the public should still be allowed to criticize it morally, she believes legalization is the best way to both safeguard women's rights and deal constructively with the social problems related to the activity.

"Li Yinhe is an interesting figure," said Lionel. "But in truth she does not represent the opinion of a majority of people." Again, no dissent.

"OK," said Kristin, nimbly switching ground. "What about the second argument. School is a good thing, right? You are all here to get a good education so you can make money and support your parents. Well," she continued, "suppose a girl who is your age can't afford to go to school. Why shouldn't she turn to prostitution to earn the money?"

"She could just save money," replied Marlene.

Ruth disagreed. "My sister had just moved to Guangdong. The best she could earn is one thousand renminbi (about $125) a month. You cannot save money for college in that job. And she has a good job."

"Well," sighed Marlene. "Not everyone can go to college. There is plenty of respectable work without a college degree."

"But is it fair to deprive these people of the right to earn as much income as those with college degrees?" I asked.

"I don't know if it is fair," replied Lionel, "but it is life."

There was one argument left, but it wasn't doing any better. "If someone wants to have sexual exploration," said Angelina, "she does not need to become a prostitute. There is plenty of opportunity."

Interestingly, just about this time the Associated Press ran a story titled "China's Sexual Revolution." The article provided some suggestive statistics, including the fact that high school girls make up 80 percent of the women getting abortions during the one-week school holiday and that 60 to 70 percent of Chinese have had sex before marriage. There was also plenty of anecdotal evidence: a twenty-year-old waitress declared that her friends often go to bars to pick up men while a young golf instructor boasted of his sexual exploits. Other signs of degeneration included mention of a bar devoted exclusively to one-night stands and hotels that rent out rooms by the hour.

I laid this evidence before the group and asked what they thought. If, as Angelina suggested, there was plenty of opportunity for sexual exploration, did this mean China was entering a period of sexual liberation like America in the sixties?

"I only meant," said Angelina, "that if a woman wanted, there was plenty of opportunity for sexual activity. Outside of our own college, there are rooms to rent by the hour. But most people go there with their boyfriends because there is no other place to be alone."

"I also think that article sensationalizes," added Marlene. "There may be a few examples like what they cite. But I do not believe that is how things are for the most part. For the most part, we follow traditional Chinese values."

"But I also think Beijing and Shanghai are very different than Chengdu," suggested Sophie.

My guess was that all of the above comments had some degree of truth in them. Magazines sensationalize, traditional Chinese values are very conservative when it comes to sex, and there are always exceptions. Of course, there exists no monolithic Chinese view on the subject. But my own sense was that while Chengdu was certainly far from the modern metropolises of Shanghai and Beijing where the article was set, in some ways this out-of-the-way region—often referred to as the breadbasket of China—offered a more meaningful perspective from which to view the culture than any of those places. It's the difference between the opinions of students at a college in New York or Los Angeles as compared to those at a state university in Nebraska. To which one, you might ask, would you turn for a more accurate representation of the real America?

NINETEEN

What Is Truth?

Some nights, the two hours we had scheduled for the discussion just flew by. Other evenings, when we would get off on some irrelevant tangent or people were particularly reluctant to engage in conversation, the clock seemed to stand still as I waited for someone, anyone, to answer a question. Tonight was definitely one of the former evenings; indeed, I do not remember the hundred and twenty minutes disappearing so quickly. This feature of time—its apparent subjectivity—is something we are all familiar with and philosophers have long commented on. Aristotle described this phenomenon in *Physics,* while Kant famously argued in *Critique of Pure Reason* that time is not an objective part of the world but is imposed on reality by human consciousness. Indeed, the nature of time would have been a great subject for its own evening. But although it was proposed time and again, it never got voted in. Many great topics did not get covered and, because my time in China was running out, would not get covered, at least by me. In a couple of months the semester would be finished, the discussion group ended, and it would be time for me to leave. Although I was gratified that Kristin was planning to continue the tradition the following year, I was more than a little saddened by all of the philosophical surfaces I would leave unscratched. The time had flown by. Had it really been nearly two years?

As we had exhausted most of the topics on my original list and students were still reluctant to propose their own ideas, I had put together a new set of questions. The one chosen for tonight was, "Does truth change from culture to culture?" Although the issue seemed to me filled with philosophical possibilities, one could never be certain how things would turn out. At least we had a good-sized audience. Indeed, if you added in the regular coffeehouse customers already filling the café tables and booths, the combined crowd would have violated the fire code, had there been one. I made sure to position myself near the door just in case.

Unfortunately, I could not take full credit for the burgeoning numbers. Nearly one-third of the group was brought along by my counterpart teacher, Wang Jiali, in what constituted another of my seemingly endless cultural lessons. I've already mentioned the notion of guanxi, the idea that doing a favor for someone entails an obligation on their part to reciprocate. It is tough enough to figure out the parameters of guanxi—for how long and to what degree this reciprocity extends. Complicating matters even further is the indirectness that is woven into the fabric of Chinese culture. It is often bad form to simply ask outright for a favor, since if for some reason the person has to refuse, he can lose face. For example, if you want a friend to help you move, rather than confronting him directly with the appeal, you might instead bring up your difficulties in making preparations for the process. Given this cue, the knowing friend, generally speaking, will volunteer to assist you if it is at all possible. Conversely, if the aforementioned acquaintance complains about some issue to you, it is quite natural to interpret the grumbling as a request for aid. So when I had griped to Wang Jiali that the sign for our discussion group had been vandalized, in my mind I was simply letting off some steam. To her, however, it was a call to arms. When she discovered that she could neither find the perpetrators nor prevent a reoccurrence, she decided to at least bring her students to the discussion as a show of support. I appreciated the gracious gesture, but the large numbers made it almost impossible to have a coherent conversation. Random exchanges kept breaking out among the participants, and I would have to ask people to repeat things so they could be heard over the noise. In the future, or what little was left of it, I vowed to be more careful with my complaints.

I started out the discussion tonight by making a distinction between two types of truth: Truth with a capital T and truth with a small t.

"We can say something is true with a capital T"— I held up a big piece of paper with "Truth" written on it—"and by this we mean that it is true for everyone at all times. For example, we use 'truth' in this capital T way when we say it is true that 2+2=4. However, it seems we use the word 'truth' in a quite different sense when we declare that truth changes from culture to culture." Here, I held up a sheet of paper with "truth" written on it. "We seem here to be using the term 'truth' with a small *t*, meaning that a culture's practice is true for it but not necessarily for any other culture. For example, there is no truth with a capital *T* about what utensils a culture should use. In China, people think chopsticks best, while Americans prefer forks and knives."

Almost immediately I feared I had made a mistake. Given the frequency with which "Can you use chopsticks?" is repeatedly asked of foreigners—even those who have resided in China for years—I realized that this analogy might have opened a can of worms. Thankfully, the reference went unnoticed. Cognizant of the Peace Corps' three T's rule (no discussing Tiananmen, Taiwan, or Tibet), for the most part I had avoided raising politics as an issue during the course of our sessions. But tonight, perhaps because my time was drawing to a close, it seemed like a good evening to crack open that Pandora's box ever so slightly. So I asked, "Now, when it comes to politics, do you think there is truth with a small *t* or truth with a capital *T*?"

As if sitting on a fastball, Pioneer, who with his philosophical training certainly understood the issues at stake better than anyone, jumped on the question. "I think on this subject most Americans believe in truth with a capital *T*. This is why they invaded Iraq, in order to spread the true political system."

"'True' with a capital *T*?" I asked.

"Yes. Certainly. At least they think it is."

"OK. But what about the Chinese? I want to know what you all think when it comes to politics. Do you believe there is a truth with a capital *T*?"

"I agree with Keats," began Lionel. "Truth is beauty and beauty is truth." I stared at him blankly, waiting for him to complete his thought. But that was it.

"You're going to have to explain that to me a little more, Lionel," I finally replied.

"What I mean," he began, "is that truth will be evident by its effects in the world. A disordered, chaotic political system will not be a true one."

"True with a small *t* or a capital *T*?" I asked.

Lionel rubbed his chin and said, "Let me think about that for a second."

Seizing the opening, Marlene declared, "I think he is saying that there is a 'Truth' with a capital *T*, but that it does not belong to any particular political system. Rather, if a system is creating order and stability, then it is the correct system for that culture or that country. But many systems can embody this."

"Yes, I agree," added Lionel.

Situated perfectly between Scylla (only one political system is the correct one) and Charybdis (all governments, even the most tyrannical, are equal), this was a classic middle way answer. It not only avoided hubris and nihilism but also allowed everyone in the room to feel good about his or her own political system. Moderate and face-saving, what wasn't there to like about it? In the West, the idea that the primary value of a political system is order and stability goes back to Plato, who believed that the ideal society was composed of three distinct classes, each performing its proper task. The current Chinese government's emphasis on the construction of a "harmonious society" (*hexie shehui*) shares Plato's preference for the smooth functioning of the whole over the self-expression of the individual.

The antithesis to harmony is not chaos but rather America—at least according to my academic supervisor at Sichuan Normal. Perhaps because he felt sorry for how little we earned compared to the other teachers, once a semester Mr. Yang would treat the two Peace Corps volunteers to an upscale restaurant. Since he coordinated programs with several American universities and visited these at least once a year, he was familiar with current events in the United States and enjoyed discussing them with us on these occasions. At our most recent get-together he was inquiring about the American presidential primaries, which were then in full swing. As we were speculating on which candidates might win their respective party's nomination, he interrupted us to offer up the following observation:

"I do not understand," he said smiling, "why you Americans put yourself through this every four years. It seems simply crazy to us Chinese. Why go through all this fighting and rancor? We had our period of chaos in China with the Cultural Revolution. No one here wants to go back to that."

I wasn't sure how many people had died in the American electoral process in the past two hundred plus years, but I was pretty certain it was significantly fewer than the three million some historians estimate perished during the Cultural Revolution. Which is not to say that he did not have a point. No one doubts that the American political system is broken. Bipartisanship is dead; politicians from either side of the aisle barely speak to each other. Were this combative attitude confined to Washington, it might not be any more damaging than a localized epidemic. Unfortunately, the virus has spread throughout the body politic, most notably with the famous red state/blue state divide. I think the fact that George W. Bush rode to victory in part on his claim to be a uniter and that Obama promised to move beyond partisanship shows a desire in the hearts of the American people to transcend our differences. But we have notoriously been unable to accomplish this. If those who disagree in a democracy cannot discuss their differences in a respectful manner but instead view each other as enemies, then the game is lost. Didn't someone once mention something about a nation divided against itself not being able to stand? In truth, a little more concern with harmony in our country would not be a bad thing. As a new convert to the Church of the Middle Way, I would suggest we seek something between Chinese uniformity and American dysfunction, though I'm not sure what that would look like.

But back to Marlene. Her answer—that any government is true so long as it brings about order and stability—may have seemed elegantly designed to mollify all sides in the debate, but it had some deficiencies. Before I could raise a few of the more obvious of these, Kristin stepped in. "What if," she asked, "the government imposes its order by repressing its people?"

I was beginning to get a little uncomfortable. Just a week prior, violent riots had broken out in Tibet on the forty-ninth anniversary of its failed uprising against Beijing's rule. Local television stations and newspapers were filled with images of Tibetans burning down buildings and attacking Chinese, while the coverage from the Western media had a decidedly more pro-Tibet slant. On nothing were our two worldviews more polarized than on the subject of the spiritual leader of Tibet, the 14th Dalai Lama. I had bitten my tongue several times while colleagues, friends, and even complete strangers had lashed out at the monk Tenzin Gyatso, not only as the instigator of the riots but as a genuinely destructive figure in human history. Was the person they described with such antipathy the same smiling monk I had often seen speak so passionately about universal love and nonviolence? The whole situation reminded me of the way that whites and blacks had viewed the O. J. Simpson murder trial verdict differently (well, the first one).

"A society that did this would not be truly ordered," Marlene shot back. "Or at least it would not maintain its order very long."

Before I could say "circular argument," Shirley jumped in. "One hundred years ago monarchy was believed to be the best political system. Now today everyone disagrees. There is no truth in politics, only opinion." Although Plato's main antagonist, Protagoras, may have said it slightly differently more than two thousand years ago, with his statement that, "Man is the measure of all things," it amounted to the same claim. That is, when it comes to politics or anything else, there is only opinion (truth with a small *t*). Ironically, the political system that Plato would develop in response to this relativism looked much more like communist China than anything we would recognize.

The two sides in the debate—those supportive of Truth (with a capital *T*) and those suspicious of its existence—now seemed joined and ready to go at it. That is, until Jiali, my counterpart teacher, jumped into the discussion. "This is supposed to be a philosophy club," she began, seeming more upset than the situation called for. "But what does politics have to do with philosophy?"

It was such an obvious non sequitur—it was so clearly not relevant to the debate that we had joined over whether or not truth exists in politics—that I had to stop for a moment and try to figure out what she meant by it. The usual reason people blurted out obviously irrelevant comments was either that they had not been listening or they simply did not understand the topic. Since I knew Jiali was both smarter and more attentive than this, the logical conclusion was that something else was going on. Suddenly a light bulb went on in my head: not only was she part of the university administration, she was a Communist Party member to boot. Having brought these students here, Jiali no doubt had some accountability to her higher ups for what they were exposed to this evening. My guess was no more than the ancient Greeks did the leaders of the local chapter of the Party appreciate corruption of the youth, although in truth over the course of these discussions the students had probably had more effect on my thinking than the other way around. I certainly didn't want to get her in trouble, but neither did I feel I could back down at this point.

"Consider the situation in Tibet," I said, finally stating openly what had been the subtext for the evening. "A lot of people in the West think that China is repressing the Tibetans while in China the situation is perceived very differently, correct?"

"This is because your news media are not reporting the situation accurately," said Jiali.

"So then our subject for tonight, truth, does have something to do with politics."

"But what does politics have to do with philosophy?"

She wasn't giving up without a fight. So I thought I would try another tack.

"Do you think China's actions in Tibet were morally correct?"

"Yes."

"So you do at least think politics has something to do with ethics?"

"Certainly."

"But ethics is a part of philosophy."

"So?"

"Well, if ethics is a part of philosophy and ethics has to do with politics, then politics obviously has something to do with philosophy."

"But what does politics has to do with the subject for tonight, truth?"

This was all having a "Who's on first, what's on second" feel to it. But I saw her strategy. While we were arguing about whether we should be discussing politics, we were not discussing politics. And she was winning.

Thankfully, Marlene jumped in to get us out of the vicious circle we seemed to be descending into. "I want to change my mind," she said. "I do not think there is absolute truth, even in science. One day something is a planet, the next day it is not," she said, referring to the recent change in the status of Pluto. "So people's opinions could change."

"What about Hitler?" I asked. "Could the opinion that Hitler was evil change?"

"I do not think it will."

"But it could."

"Yes. I guess it could."

"But just because the opinions change does not mean the truth has to change," I replied.

"What do you mean?" she asked.

"Well, whether people define Pluto as a planet might change. But that doesn't mean the laws of nature change. Or if people stopped believing in evolution, that would not make evolution false. Human opinion can change while truth remains the same."

While Marlene and the rest of the group were thinking this over, Lionel decided to rejoin the conversation. "I don't agree with either of you. I don't think truth is something we can use to make absolute judgments. But neither do I agree with Marlene that truth changes from age to age. I think it is like light from a distant star. It is something we are trying to reach, but perhaps never will."

"Can you give me an example?"

"The phrase 'of the people, for the people, by the people' represents an ideal for both the Chinese and the American. But I do not think we have reached it."

This certainly wasn't a line of thinking I had been expecting to hear—a Chinese student invoking Thomas Jefferson to argue for moral parity between communism and democracy.

"What do you mean?" I asked.

"Right now in China, average citizens have little actual input into choosing their leadership. But direct election is a goal of the Communist Party."

"And what about America? You said we had fallen short of that ideal."

As if suddenly realizing that it would be bad form to point out another nation's deficiency, he replied, "Well maybe I was wrong. Perhaps you have reached your ideal."

"I hope not," I said, and meant it. All he was asking for was a shared humility between our two nations, but I don't think he realized what he was up against. I would have to break it to him.

"Look," I said. "For better or worse, most Americans don't view truth as light from a distant star. Think of Thomas Jefferson. 'Truth,' Jefferson has written in the Declaration of Independence, 'is self-evident,' at least the truth that all men are created equal and endowed with certain inalienable rights. Most Americans view truth like this, as something that can be acquired and used as a basis for action."

"So President Bush went into Iraq because all men are created equal?" inquired Pioneer.

"In fact this was part of his rationale. He argued Iraqis deserved freedom like all human beings. So he was going there to bring it to them." Here was the dark side of my China personality emerging again.

"And it had nothing to do with oil?" he asked.

I backed down. "I'm not saying I agree with him. Most Americans, you know, are against the war. I'm just telling you what he said."

"In China," added Lionel, "we believe in the doctrine of 'non-interference.' Countries should be allowed to pursue their policies without hindrance from other nations." Although this was the official government policy, I had a feeling Lionel was bringing it up not to enlighten me on this matter but to implicitly reply to my earlier remarks about Tibet. It was as if he were saying, "Believe in Truth with a capital *T* all you want, but Tibet is no business of yours."

Fortunately for Jiali I had no desire to push this issue any further, though here it is interesting to speculate on the relation between metaphysics and politics, since both the invasion of Iraq and the claim of non-interference in Tibet have philosophical roots that go back thousands of years. The very first passage of the Bible's Gospel of John identifies God with *logos*, or reason. As a result of this connection, human rationality has access to a whole slew of truths, from "It's wrong to covet thy neighbor's wife" to "It's permissible to stone homosexuals." And if moral truth is knowable, can political truth be far behind? By contrast, the *Tao Te Ching* begins with the claim that the Tao that can be spoken of is not the actual Tao, that is, that the Tao is beyond reason and apprehension. If reason is limited and ultimate truth unattainable, then caution and humility are the appropriate responses. Indeed, anyone who wants to understand the Chinese attitude toward human rights will have to begin with the realization that it is as much metaphysical as anything else. The whole language of human rights is tied to the notion of Truth with a capital *T*, a concept that does not have a strong foothold anywhere in Chinese intellectual history.

"It seems you and Marlene at least agree that absolute truth is not knowable."

"Yes," said Marlene. "Maybe someone who believes he has absolute truth is a danger. I think Hitler believed in Truth with a capital *T*."

One of Jiali's students who had been standing in the back of the room all night spoke up. "I am having a hard time following the conversation," she admitted. "So can you tell me what the answer is?"

"The answer to what?" I asked.

"The answer to the question, what is truth? Is it with a capital *T* or small *t*?"

I didn't know where to begin. It was a question I would be asked not infrequently in an Introduction to Philosophy class back in the States. After a vigorous debate on the existence of God or the morality of torture, students would often ask me to resolve the controversy by providing the correct answer. Many were disappointed when I told them I didn't know the truth, and a few got downright angry when I said neither did I think anyone else did. It was the debate that really mattered. This idea is hardly original. Socrates went to his grave con-fessing that the only thing he knew was that he didn't know anything. Come to think of it, there was something very Taoist about that claim.

As I was contemplating how to respond, Sophie jumped in: "We do not come here to get answers," she said. "We are here for the sake of discussion."

"Yes," echoed Marlene. "This is philosophy."

I couldn't have said it better myself.

TWENTY

Meltdown

When I try to piece together why it happened, I first blame myself, since it was my action that resulted in the request that our discussion group not returning to the Macchiato Café. But in my defense, I would bring up a very, very short film I once saw titled *Death of a Rat*. The film opens with a man being chewed out by his boss. When the man arrives home, he screams at his wife, who yells at their kid, who hits the dog, who chases the cat, who gruesomely brings about the demise of the film's title character. Just so, I would suggest that the chain of events that culminated in my "meltdown," as I like to call it, was as inevitable as it was inappropriate. If, as philosophers say, responsibility requires the ability to do other than one actually does, then I am not sure that in a technical sense I could be held fully accountable for what occurred that evening.

Let's just say that the situation was complicated, and that the surface depiction of events would not tell the entire story. For example, despite appearances, the whole thing had nothing to do with the café customer listening to a transistor radio. He was what Aristotle would have called the "efficient" cause, that is, the motivating factor closest to the event in time. True, if he had turned the damn thing down the third or fourth time I had asked him, I would not have had to jump out of my chair, rush across the room, and engage in the action that ultimately got us exiled. But I doubt that the senseless noise emanating from his radio would have bothered me so much had it not been for the senseless noise I had been hearing from a few people's mouths that evening. It was exclusively from new people, and it was mostly stuff I had heard countless times before, involving allegations that American parents routinely require children over eighteen to pay rent or move out, and that the children reciprocate by essentially abandoning their elders to the wolves once they reach retirement age. And it wasn't the assertions as much as the flimsy evidence cited to justify them that gave me the headache. Isolated news reports, testimony from a friend, or the words "everyone knows that" were the most common grounding for these claims. There was even a new angle added to the anti-American barrage involving the movie *Saving Private Ryan*. Far from depicting something praiseworthy, the film, I was informed, actually illustrated a peculiarly American vice, since the massive efforts put forth to retrieve the remaining Ryan sibling privileged the individual over the group.

I doubt the lies and distortions about my country would have troubled me so much had it not been that for the past two weeks I had been subjected to falsification on a scale that I had not personally witnessed in my lifetime, or at least since Watergate. I am referring, of course, to the Chinese media's coverage of the Tibet riots. Although the actual fighting in the streets of Lhasa had quieted down, controversy still raged. One hotly debated issue involved a CNN photograph of the riots showing Chinese military vehicles hunting down an unarmed Tibetan. Although unlikely to be featured in a national tourist board ad, the picture nevertheless became a rallying cry for Chinese nationalism when it was revealed that CNN had cropped the image so as to exclude the detail that the police themselves had been under attack by protestors. According to every Chinese with access to the Internet, this was evidence of a Western conspiracy to make China look bad to the rest of the world just months before the Olympics were scheduled to begin.

Of course, it was hard to find out exactly what was happening in Tibet because the border had been shut down and no reporters were allowed in. Instead, the Chinese media ran a continuous video loop that could be titled "Monks Gone Wild," focusing not on the use of police force against Tibetans but exclusively on the ethnic Chinese that had been killed during the riot. All the while, Premier Wen Jiabao accused the Dalai Lama of being the mastermind behind the uprising. If you were to believe the news, the monks were solely responsible for the carnage, the Dalai Lama was the instigator, the Chinese police had acted with great restraint, and the Western media had manipulated the facts.

Now I am not sure which one of those statements was the biggest fabrication; indeed, it might have been a toss-up. This is not to say that when it comes to the situation in Tibet, one group can claim to be on the side of the angels. True, China invaded the country and chased the Dalai Lama out more than a half century ago. But their claim to what is known as the Tibetan Autonomous Region is recognized by most countries. Even the Dalai Lama acknowledges Chinese authority in Tibet and does not seek independence. China itself asserts, not without justification, that it has modernized what was a backward society. But one can also understand the nervousness of the Tibetans when thousands upon thousands of ethnic Chinese pour into the region threatening to deprive them of economic opportunity. And anyone who thinks religious freedom exists anywhere in China only need to Google "Falun Gong," the combination of Buddhism and Taoism, followers of which are regularly imprisoned.

All of this provides a pretty good rationale for the Peace Corps policy on political expression, which more or less boils down to "just say no to discussing politics." While the Peace Corps places no explicit restrictions on volunteer speech, we are in essence asked to check our political views at the border. There are a couple of good reasons for this. First, since we are there at the request of the host country, it seems bad form to insult those who have invited us by questioning the legitimacy of their political institutions, just like you wouldn't ask someone who was treating you to a meal whether they were using counterfeit currency to pay the bill. Moreover, our role as unofficial ambassadors of goodwill on behalf of the United States government would be compromised, to say the least, if we spent all our time arguing and irritating people. In fact, the limitations actually are not as burdensome as they might appear, since most of the volunteers are recent college graduates with surprisingly little sense of history and at best fleeting interest in contemporary events.

In practice, every volunteer I knew made a clear distinction between the Chinese people and the Chinese government. Regardless of what we thought about the actions of the Chinese government, we loved our Chinese host families, who took us in for our first few months in the country. We loved the cities we were assigned to and their residents, who invariably performed innumerable random acts of kindness, from inviting us to tea to giving us their seats on the bus to helping us when we were lost. We loved our students, who were grateful we had come so far to teach them, if confused about why we would do so for free. We loved the language, the culture, the landscape. It is impossible to spend any length of time in China and not become enamored of the country and its people.

At least for me, the Tibet riots tore down this curtain between the Chinese people and the Chinese government. What I saw—what I did not want to see but could not help but see—were people I respected and admired supporting what seemed to me to be ruthless repression by their government. While at one level I always knew that this division between the people and their leaders was not as clean as I had imagined it, on another level it was like the joke about Einstein not speaking until he was five years old. Asked why, after a half decade, he suddenly blurted out at breakfast one morning that "the toast is cold," young Albert replied that up until that point, everything had been all right. Just so, my time in China seemed to correspond with a relatively benign period in China's relationship with other nations. Without any major flare-ups that might have brought forth international condemnation and provoked the expected response from its citizens, I could focus on the one side of the equation I wanted to see.

In a real sense, the divergent reactions to the Tibet protest reminded me of the abortion debate in America. In the discussion over the Tibet riots, each side brought certain cultural assumptions to the table and as a result viewed the same set of facts very differently. Under these conditions, argument made no sense, since people were past the point of being able to be persuaded. The best that could be hoped for, it seemed, was that through listening one could gain insight into the other side's point of view. So, since I could neither confront the lies I had been hearing on Tibet because of the Peace Corps policy on politics, nor dispel the falsehoods being told about my country (not only tonight but over the course of the last two years because, well, because it would have no effect and people would go on believing what they are told), and in short, because I felt I was drowning in a sea of lies, I screamed at a guy listening to a transistor radio to turn the damn thing down or I was going to shove it up his ass.

Despite the fact that the recipient of the request probably understood not a word of what was being asked of him, I immediately regretted my outburst. Not only was it a completely illogical act for reasons I've just enumerated. More important, the last thing one does in China—even worse than killing someone, I think—is to openly express anger. I'm pretty sure you could commit murder with a calmness the Chinese would find admirable. But there is no way in China to lose your temper and keep your face. And so it came as no surprise when, shortly after the discussion ended, it was conveyed to me—in a very face-saving manner—that it might be best for us to hold our meetings at another location.

In retrospect I can understand why I reacted as I did, though I can't excuse it. Of course, it seems more than a little ironic that in reacting to one stereotype I had created another. On more than one occasion I had encountered blanket generalizations about my countrymen based on a single incident blown out of proportion. Someone had once heard about an American woman who had re-fused to reciprocate in sharing food with her Chinese roommate. As a result, countless numbers of my students had become convinced that all Americans are stingy. Heretofore, numerous Chinese would confidently assert that Americans easily lose their temper and as justification they would appeal to a tale about the unprompted ravings of a foreign teacher.

If they hadn't dissed the Dalai Lama, though, it might never have come to this. So in a way, I guess, I find myself in the same place as the Chinese leader-ship. We both blame the spiritual leader of Tibet for a messy situation.

Oh yes, the topic for the evening? As you might be able to guess, I didn't take very good notes.

TWENTY-ONE

What Is Gender?

Fortunately, word did not spread very quickly at the open-air mall at the south gate of campus. Or if it did, the owner of the third and final establishment to host our weekly meetings was either oblivious to it or simply happy for our business. In either case, the move had been fortuitous. National Public Radio was going to be featuring a week of live broadcasts from Chengdu. Directed our way by the Peace Corps China office, Andrea Hsu, a producer from the show *All Things Considered,* was scheduled to sit in on the upcoming session of our discussion in order to decide if a segment on us would be worthy for inclusion on the show. Because of its cramped and noisy environs, the Macchiato Café would have been a less than ideal environment for our audition. By contrast, the owner of You Love Coffee had cordoned off a section of the establishment away from the regular customers so we would be able to conduct our business in a relatively undisturbed manner. On second thought, maybe our reputation had preceded us.

In either case, I had more than the usual anxiety when it came to choosing a topic for this session, since a good discussion could land us possible air time, while a dud would mean a one-way ticket to Palookaville, or its Chinese equivalent. The problem was that there seemed no obvious correlation between the choice of subject and the intensity of the debate. Great exchanges often flowed from what seemed to me to be trivial or misguided issues, while some of the hot-button ones just fell flat. Hence, I decided to forgo handing out the usual list of suggestions and put the burden on the group to determine the question for the evening. This, I reasoned, had as good a chance as anything of arriving at something that might work. However, after the votes had been cast, I quickly began to reconsider the wisdom of my maneuver.

It's not that a discussion about transsexuals didn't hold out the hope of taking us to some interesting philosophical places. It was just that I wasn't sure they were places I was comfortable going. However, it did promise a welcome diversion from the tension of the last few sessions. The topic had been in the news of late because of an American, Thomas Beattie, the pregnant woman turned man. Although, as I have stated, one could never be certain precisely what stories from America the Chinese media would cover, a news cycle devoted to Thomas Beattie was not unexpected. Sure, it did not evidence Americans killing each other or abusing our parents. But violating the norms of nature was enough of a sign of cultural decay to warrant attention. It seems as well a popular Chinese television show on which people in difficulty asked the public for donations had recently featured a couple of pre-op transsexuals pleading for funds.

At first I had downplayed the significance of having NPR do a segment on our discussion group. In truth, a five-minute segment on public radio was hardly worth getting worked up about. As that great "philosopher" Humphrey Bogart might have said, it didn't amount to a hill of beans in this crazy world. However, I had given nearly two years of my life to teaching in China. It would naturally have been gratifying to have one of the fruits of this effort broadcast around the country. In addition, I reasoned that getting the American public, or at least NPR's slice of it, to listen to a segment on the lively clash of ideas among Chinese undergraduates—speaking in English no less—might help to dispel the impression of the Chinese as an intellectually monolithic people and, hence, further the Peace Corps goal of fostering understanding among nations. OK, maybe I just wanted my fifteen minutes of NPR fame.

First, however, the topic had to be tweaked a little. If transsexualism did not pass the two-thousand-year rule—since even as advanced as ancient Chinese medicine might have been, they weren't doing those sorts of operations— gender certainly did. Gender roles have been around as long as humans, and a discussion of their nature and usefulness would, I reasoned, more than fill up the allotted time and might even get us on the air. I broke the subject into two distinct sections. First, we would consider whether gender roles are inherent in nature or are socially constructed. Second, we would ask what, if anything, the phenomenon of transexualism indicates about the nature of gender.

Pioneer began the evening with a philosophical discourse that I could tell he had elaborately prepared because he was reading from notes. "In China, we have the notion of yin and yang. These concepts are recognition of an inherent conflict in the nature of reality, but a conflict whose two sides are connected. Yin is related to dark and night, while yang is associated with day and sun. Day and night are obviously opposites. But they just as obviously require each other. It is the same with man and woman. We have two different natures, but man and woman need each other."

"So it sounds like you want to say that gender roles are natural."

"Yes."

"And what do you think about transsexuals?" I asked.

"It is very strange," he replied, shaking his head. "I do not think it is good for our society."

Before I could ask him why, Marlene jumped in. "I agree that that there are two different natures. Women are *wenrou* and *shanliang*, gentle and kind. Men are more aggressive. This is nature."

"But why do you think these are natural, Marlene?" Kristin jumped in. "Don't Chinese boys play with soldiers and girls with dolls? So how do you know this is not a result of training?"

"Men were aggressive before there were toy soldiers. And there are many other differences. Men are better at math."

"I know a lot of girls who are good at math," replied Kristin.

"I only mean it is true for the most part. I also think that for the most part men are better politicians than women because they are more cunning and ruthless. The same is true in the business world. Men have more what it takes to succeed there."

"But there have been plenty of women in Chinese history at least as cunning and ruthless as any man," Sophie chimed in. "Just like in America."

"Yes," added Lionel. "This is what makes Hillary Clinton a good leader." He paused. "But for the most part, leaders have been men."

"Indira Ghandi? Golda Maier? Margaret Thatcher? Come on," I said.

"I mean in China," said Lionel.

"What about Wu Zetian?" Angelina chimed in.

"Who?" I asked.

"China's only female emperor," added Sophie.

"I said 'for the most part,'" replied Lionel.

"Besides," added Marlene. "These women succeeded because they acted according to the male or yang nature."

"Let me see if I have this straight," I said. "Marlene, you want to say men and women have different natures but that the male nature is necessary for success in politics and business. And when women succeed it is because they lose their nature and imitate that of the male."

"Yes."

"And Sophie, you think there is no female or male nature."

"No, I agree with what has been said, that there is a female nature. I just don't think it has anything to do with success at math or business or politics. Women will succeed in these areas when they are given the opportunity."

"Does anyone think men and women have the same nature?"

Kristin, the American Peace Corps volunteer, was the only person who raised her hand.

"What does this have to do with transsexuals?" asked Pioneer.

"Well," I said, wondering myself, "someone might say that the transsexuals featured on television have a female nature that has been put in a male body. But if they were just trying to get into their natural role, would they not be acting in accord with nature?"

"I guess," he concluded, "that if they are trying to achieve their true nature, this is something we should tolerate."

In thus changing his attitude toward transsexuals, Pioneer seemed to drive home a point about the difference between Chinese philosophy and the Judeo-Christian world picture. If you believe in God, then you not only accept the notion of male and female natures but also believe that one could not have been assigned the wrong nature, as transsexuals claimed to have been, because, well, doing anything wrong is not very God-like. By contrast, without a divine being, Chinese philosophy is free to accept all the mistakes it wants. Moreover, as I've already pointed out, Taoism is all about opposites changing into each other. What is more in this spirit of transformation than a man becoming a woman? That said, it would just be wrong to assume that this sentiment is shared by any large percentage of the Chinese population. It's just that Pioneer, like any philosopher, was consistent in following out the implications of a worldview.

"If a transsexual is someone who wants to be in the other sex's body, does that mean I should be a transsexual?" interjected Ruth. I had no idea where this was going to go. She continued, "When I was growing up, I wanted to be a boy." At first, I could not tell whether she was joking or dead serious.

"What do you mean?" I asked. "Did you like playing with dolls?"

"Yes."

"Did you feel more comfortable around boys?"

"No."

"Then why did you want to be a boy?"

"Because my brother was allowed to do things and go places I was not."

"I don't think that is quite the same," I tried to explain. "The transsexual feels that they are in the wrong body. It doesn't seem to me this is how you felt."

"Oh," she said, slightly embarrassed.

There was a long, awkward silence. I thought of the claim I had heard numerous times in China that having a girl is like watering someone else's garden, and the unimaginable consequences of this sentiment being repeated millions of times for thousands of years.

"Where does the *kongque* man fit in?" asked Marlene.

"What?" I said. We seemed to be bouncing around all over the place now.

"The peacock men," translated Angelina, who went on to describe what seemed to me to be roughly the equivalent of metrosexuals, young men who were especially concerned with personal adornment and style.

"What do you think?" I asked. "Is this some third nature, neither male nor female?"

"Most people do not accept this," replied Angelina.

"I disagree," said Marlene. "Our parents' generation is against this, just like it is against transsexuals. But many young people feel differently."

"What about in this room?" I asked. "How many people support transsexuals in getting an operation?"

Nearly three quarters raised their hands.

"Why?"

"This is their dream," said Marlene. "We should all follow our dream."

Isn't that the American dream?

I was proud of the group. They had handled a controversial issue with intelligence and insight, putting forth a variety of perspectives and engaging in a lively and respectful debate. And just as Ginger Rogers did everything Fred Astaire did but backward and in high heels, so these students had carried this all out in a second language. I thought we were a shoe-in for the big show. But recalling how the lost horse story reminds us that we can never be certain about the outcome of an event, I braced myself—and so was not completely caught off guard a couple of days later when Andrea e-mailed to regretfully inform me that as much as she enjoyed the discussion, the English-speaking level of most the group's members was not up to NPR standards for a radio broadcast.

Good news, bad news—who can tell?

TWENTY-TWO

When Is a Boycott Justified?

After the brief lull with the transexualism debate, things were heating up again at the discussion group and in China. Protests over the riots in Tibet had spread across the globe. Right about this time, the Olympic torch was making its way around the world in preparation for the Games in Beijing that summer. During its procession through France, the relay had been interrupted by protesters who had succeeded in extinguishing the torch three times. Now, members of the Republican Party had 1.4 billion converts to their France-hating club. Since nothing known as French fries existed for Chinese to rename, a movement to boycott the French department store Carrefour began to take off around China. Fanning the protests were rumors, which turned out to untrue, that a major shareholder of Carrefour had donated to the Dalai Lama.

Chinese netizens were speaking with one very offended voice on this issue. As a show of solidarity, many had not only started putting the character "heart" and the word "China" in front of their chat names, but also pressuring those who did not to follow suit. Meanwhile, the Chinese government, which could have tamped down the emotion, only made things worse by threatening serious consequences should any country follow through on a proposed boycott of the opening ceremony. That bastion of reason, CNN's Jack Cafferty, managed to exacerbate things further by referring to the Chinese leadership as "goons and thugs" in an on-air editorial. As my friend Li Juan explained it to me, since the Chinese media is controlled by the government, they assume that American media is too, and hence that the uttering of those words had the sanction of U.S.

authorities. Ultimately, CNN did offer an "apology," in which they claimed that Cafferty was referring not to the Chinese people but to their leadership. As you might imagine, that went over real big here.

In one sense, this rising tide of patriotism was to be expected. When a group feels threatened, it is only natural for a circle-the-wagons mentality to take hold. Complicating the situation in this case, however, was that the normal level of Chinese love for country hovered somewhere around where it had been in America in the days following 9/11. Little did I suspect that this emotion could actually be ratcheted up a notch or two. But the events of the last few weeks had created a situation of nationalism on steroids. Against this backdrop I was understandably a little nervous when the group voted the boycott against Carrefour as the subject for an evening's discussion.

I began that night by pointing out there are a number of reasons one might not buy products from a store. You might think the prices are too high, for example, or dislike the quality of their goods. But a boycott is different. In the case of a boycott, you specifically do not frequent a business because you think they have done something wrong, and you wish to express your displeasure. In addition, it is also usually the case that you hope some practice at the store will change as a result of your action. For example, I pointed out that when I first arrived in China, a boycott of American fast food restaurants had been undertaken on account of the low wages being paid to Chinese workers. In that case, the consumers not only wanted to punish these businesses for some perceived wrong, but they also wished to change future behavior by achieving higher pay for the employees.

I concluded, "So with the Carrefour boycott, it seems there are two things we need to ask. First, what wrong has Carrefour done that they deserve a boycott and second, what practice do you hope to change as a result of the boycott?"

I had a pretty good idea about what the first reply would be and waited.

Sure enough, a young man I had not seen before brought up the claim that one of the major shareholders in Carrefour had contributed large sums of money to the Dalai Lama.

"OK," I said, wanting to spell things out very clearly. "If this is true, this would seem to provide a moral reason for the boycott. The business or its shareholders is doing something you perceive as wrong. What behavior or practice do you hope to change by this boycott?"

Before anyone could supply the obvious answer, Lionel jumped in. "That was reported," he said. "But it was not true. No one on the board of Carrefour is giving money to the Dalai Lama."

"How do you know?

"I have been reading about the situation."

"Well, so have I," came the response from the young man who initially uttered the accusation. "And I have read that this is true."

I couldn't contain myself. "Lionel's right," I shot back, and immediately realized my mistake. If the case against the boycott was going to stick, it would have to come from the students themselves; I could have nothing to do with it. Indeed, my expression of a point of view on the complicity of Carrefour's shareholders might well threaten an honest resolution of the subject. Fortunately, some other students were informed enough about the situation to put the rumor to rest. We could move on.

"So if we can't invoke the actions of Carrefour's board of directors, what might justify the boycott?"

"In my opinion," said Lionel, "it was the actions of the French government in not protecting the torch that is the reason for the boycott."

"Yes," added Marlene, "and the French president has threatened not to come to the opening ceremonies."

"But why punish a private entity for the practices of their government? Is that any different from those who targeted innocent civilians on 9/11 because of the actions of the U.S. government?"

"A business is not the same as individuals," replied Sophie.

"True enough," I said. "But if you are angry at the French government, wouldn't it make more sense to march on the French embassy? That's what happened when the Americans accidentally bombed the Chinese embassy in Yugoslavia."

"Yes," said Lionel. "Logically, that would make more sense."

"I disagree," said Sophie. "It is not the French government we are angry at but the French people. It is the French people who disrupted the torch."

"But shouldn't you distinguish between a people and a private enterprise like Carrefour?"

"But Carrefour is run by French citizens," she replied.

"None of whom interrupted the torch relay," I said, "and all of the members of the board of Carrefour condemned the protests, is that not right?"

Silence.

Marlene jumped in. "Perhaps philosophically it cannot be justified. But I still think it was a good idea."

"Why?"

"As Sophie said, we are all very angry. We have to express this somehow."

"So how many people support the boycott of Carrefour?"

All but Angelina, who had been uncharacteristically quiet, raised their hands. I couldn't help but put her on the spot by asking for her thoughts.

"I think the whole thing is silly, even degrading for China. Everyone has already admitted there is no reason for the boycott. Yet people go ahead and do it, like sheep, because everyone is pressuring them."

"Not everyone supports the boycott," said Ren Yuan. "My father is a cab driver. And the cab drivers were against the boycott. They thought it might hurt China economically. So many went into Carrefour on the day of the boycott and bought things."

"Well, then cab drivers have better brains than college students," said Angelina. She wasn't making any friends tonight.

"No one pressured me to support the boycott," shot back the young man who had earlier claimed that Carrefour had given donations to the Dalai Lama.

"I do not think it is helpful to question the intelligence of your fellow students," added Lionel in a rare, chastising manner.

Someone else said something to Angelina in Chinese to which she sharply replied. Things seemed to be starting to turn ugly, so I tried to change the subject.

"Let's talk about what the cab drivers did, buying things at Carrefour on the day of the boycott. Are you, like them, at all worried that a boycott of Carrefour might hurt China economically? After all, Carrefour employs a lot of Chinese."

"I do not think they will pull out," said Marlene, "since they want to make money. And if they do not pull out, they will have to hire Chinese. Besides," she added, "the boycott was only for a day."

"So you would not support a longer boycott?"

"No," she replied.

"How about everyone else?"

Most sided with Marlene, although opinions ranged from Angelina's "This is stupid" to the new guy's "Death to foreigners."

In fact the government, sensing that the antiforeign sentiment being generated by the boycott and the corresponding protests in front of Carrefour was not the best public relations scheme for a country that was about to host the Olympics, would soon begin to tone it down, first warning students about keeping the protests peaceful and acting rationally and ultimately pulling the plug on the whole thing by coming out against the boycott. Interestingly, during this period it seemed very important for students to demonstrate to me that they were not mindlessly walking in lockstep with the government. I cannot count the number of times undergraduates had informed me that although they whole heartedly supported the government in this situation, they were opposed to the crackdown in Tiananmen Square. Granted, most had been pre-verbal in 1989. This was not the point. Instead, I was supposed to conclude that reason and independent thinking, not blind obedience, had led them to their current stance. I hoped they were right.

Right about now, as well, the t-shirts started to appear. They were simple white t-shirts with the phrase "I Heart China" inscribed on them, with a heart symbol instead of the word. They were sold by makeshift vendors at the gates of the college, in front of shops and around town. Every day more and more college students were donning them; they were the new black. For comparison, it is hard to imagine, even in the darkest days after 9/11, a similar trend taking hold on American college campuses.

Then there was the story of Grace Wang, a Chinese undergraduate at Duke who had been photographed trying to mediate a protest there between pro-Tibet factions and Chinese students on campus. The photograph and accompanying story circulated around the web, transforming her into a source of universal scorn among Chinese netizens, with the *New York Times* reporting that typical of the sort of response being generated was an e-mail declaring that "if you return to China, your dead corpse will be chopped into 10,000 pieces." I think it was the "Love, Mom" signature that hurt the worst. Faced with threats, her family back in China ultimately had to go into hiding. (I was just kidding about the Mom signature but not about the death threats.) To add insult to injury, her high school even revoked her diploma. Although no one among the group tonight tried to justify the backlash against her and her family (indeed, most thought these reports were fabricated), neither was there any sympathy for her efforts to try to get the two sides in this controversy to talk to each other.

All in all, reason seemed to be taking a holiday here. Having lived through America in the days, weeks, months, and years after 9/11, I felt like I had seen this story before, although I could not possibly have seen what was coming next.

TWENTY-THREE

What Is Our Obligation in a Disaster?

M onday, May 12, started like any other school day. I taught a couple of morning classes, had the lunch special at the *waiban* cafeteria, took my usual nap, and got on the bus to go for an afternoon workout at a new gym that had opened near campus. Despite claims by others of premonitions of the impending disaster—everything from frogs moving en masse to strange behavior exhibited by barnyard animals—I sensed nothing different about the day. I imagine the people of Pompeii had the same feeling of normalcy in the hours before Vesuvius blew.

Getting off the bus, I crossed the street and approached the shopping center that housed the gym when suddenly hundreds of people came streaming out of the front doors of the building and ran screaming into the street. Although I am usually not one to follow a crowd, in this case it seemed like the wise course of action. If you had asked me in mid-sprint what I thought was going on, well, I probably wouldn't have answered but would have kept running. But if you had inquired again after I had stopped to catch my breath a couple of hundred yards down the road, I would have hypothesized a Twin Towers–type building collapse to be the most likely scenario. Glancing back, however, I saw that the shopping center was still standing and showing no imminent signs of implosion. Unfortunately, my attempts to discover a cause for the obvious state of panic were yielding terms not in my Chinese vocabulary, though today I can safely say that if I forget all of the Chinese I learned, the last word that will slip from memory will be *dizheng*—earthquake.

In all honesty, I had no clue at the time that this was the cause of the panic. True, I did feel some movement below my feet, but I attributed this to a large amount of traffic and questionable construction practices, not to an 8.0 magnitude quake. Taking the bus home was one of the most surreal experiences of my life and left me with images still burned in my memory: patients from a nearby hospital being spread helter-skelter across the sidewalk; buildings and apartments emptied of customers and residents, who lined the streets as if waiting for a parade; multiple lanes of traffic heading off in every possible direction. But during the duration of my trip back to campus I had witnessed no major damage and thought, "Thank goodness."

Back at SNU, students mulled around in packs and excitedly exchanged stories of their experiences. I went to my apartment complex and found Kristin, the other Peace Corps volunteer. Although during training the Peace Corps had provided us with an emergency plan, neither of us possessed more than the vaguest recollection of what it required, except that in the worst-case scenario we were supposed to be picked up by a helicopter at the school soccer field. Since it was impossible to get through a phone call or text message, we waited for some word on our next move. In the meantime, I began to get firsthand accounts of what it felt like to be trapped inside of an apartment or classroom during an 8.0 magnitude quake, and I was thankful I had shelled out the money for the gym membership that had gotten me out of my room.

At first, an almost festive mood seemed to spread across campus, a result of the collective realization of the bullet we had dodged. It wasn't long, however, before the true nature of the disaster began to be known, and a much more somber atmosphere took hold. The epicenter of the quake, it turned out, had been a mere sixty miles away. Buildings had collapsed, whole towns had been devastated and, most tragically, countless children had been crushed inside schools. As radios blared in Chinese and those with wireless scrambled to get a connection, the reported number of dead kept increasing. Ultimately, it would reach more than eighty thousand.

Later that day we were briefly allowed back in our apartments to grab a few things, and I had a chance to observe the upheaval that had occurred in my personal space. Shelves had been emptied, furniture had shifted, and the contents of my kitchen had spilled onto the floor forming one indistinguishable mass. Had those cracks in the wall been there before or not? I could not recall. For the next five days Kristin and I were given accommodations on the first floor of the university hotel. Students were not so lucky; most camped out on the soccer field (so much for our helicopter ride) or elsewhere around campus. Indeed, Chengdu became one big tent city as even those whose homes were not damaged thought it best to sleep outside.

Classes were cancelled for the rest of the week as the campus—and the country—tried to regroup. Finally, word came that it was safe to return to our living quarters. Just as things were starting to acquire some semblance of normality, we were all awakened around eleven p.m. one evening and told to immediately evacuate our residences because a major aftershock had been predicted. Protestations that one can neither predict an earthquake or an aftershock with any meaningful degree of specificity went unheeded, and we were forced to spend the night on the first floor of a nearby building, which for some reason was deemed to be a safe location despite the fact that it sat under six stories. And then, in one of the most innovative cases of turning necessity into a virtue that I have witnessed, Chinese authorities decided to commemorate the one-week anniversary of the quake by having cars blare their horns at the precise moment the quake had struck, knowing full well that a moment of silence was no more of a realistic possibility here than time travel.

Classes resumed a few days later. Even after buildings had been declared safe, many students refused to return to their dorms or classrooms. Finally, measures had to be taken to threaten forcible removal of anyone who was still camping out on the soccer field. I was doubtful we would finish the semester. A few years ago, the Peace Corps had evacuated all of its volunteers on account of the SARS epidemic. Would that be our fate? I was certain at least that I had seen the last of our philosophy discussion group. Fortunately, we were able to put together one last session.

The topic of the final philosophical discussion, fittingly enough, was, "What is our obligation in a disaster?" I had been motivated in part by a recent editorial in the *New York Times*. An American professor teaching political theory at a prestigious Chinese university had pressed his students to consider the relative merits of spending relief money on their own country's citizens versus helping those in other nations. Using John Rawls's theory that one has a special responsibility to the worst-off members of a community, he put forward the idea that the whole world was our community so we might have a duty to other nations that superseded that to our fellow countrymen. If that was correct, then since the most recent cyclone in Burma had caused more death and destruction than the Sichuan earthquake, it might be the case that the relief funds intended for China should go to Burma instead. In the editorial, the professor had reported that he had found near universal disdain for this idea among his students. How, I wondered, would it fare here? I decided to approach the issue indirectly, asking my group of students whether there was a moral imperative for other nations to come to China's aid at this time of need.

"First, I want to say that China can deal with the situation itself," said an excited young man whose name I could not recall. "We do not need the help of other nations to take care of our country." This sentiment was resoundingly echoed by everyone in the room. It was a stark reminder that nationalism, which had been at a fever pitch before the quake, had gone into overdrive in its aftermath. To be sure, this was a natural enough response for a country to exhibit after a disaster—witness America in the days after 9/11. One indicator of this uptick in patriotic fervor was the increased sales of the "I Heart China" t-shirts. Although they had sold well since their introduction in the aftermath of the Tibet riots and the Carrefour boycott, these shirts were now being ordered by entire classes, and shopkeepers were reporting they could not keep them in stock.

"OK," I replied. "But even if you don't need it, do other nations have an obligation to offer aid to China at this time?"

"It is a nice gesture," said Lionel. "But no, I would not say it is morally required."

"I think if other nations give to China, they do so out of self-interest," added Sophie, "either because China has helped other nations and they want that aid to continue, or China has resources that other nations desire."

There followed a rather extensive list of nations and corporations and what they had so far donated. Some had been generous, while others had obviously failed to meet expectations. It was clear the students thought there should be consequences. I was reminded of nothing so much as my mother, who knew without ever recording it on a piece of paper how much every friend and relative had given to her children's weddings, anniversaries, and assorted graduations, and based her own giving accordingly. This was guanxi writ large.

"So," I asked, "if other nations are under no obligation to assist China in this time of need, does this mean China has no duty toward other similarly situated nations?"

"China already gives plenty of aid," replied Sophie.

In the just-mentioned editorial, the professor, a political scientist, had backed off once he sensed resistance on the part of the students to the notion of China having to provide aid to other nations at this time of its own need, and he even sent an e-mail to his students apologizing for his insensitivity. This, I think, is a difference between philosophy and all other academic disciplines. When things get intellectually uncomfortable, we don't retreat but instead feel compelled to push forward and investigate claims, explore underlying assumptions, and analyze proposed justifications. We like to think we are being advocates for the truth, though in fact we might just be asses; it's a fine line. In any case, it was time to play the role philosophers have been carrying out since Socrates and hope there was no hemlock nearby.

"Suppose," I said, "you could spend relief money either to save the life of a Burmese child or save the leg of a Chinese child. Where should the money be spent?"

I was not sure whether the silence indicated they were seriously considering the question or could not believe I had made such an inquiry. Finally, Lionel spoke up: "In this case, I would vote to save the leg of the Chinese child." His answer was quickly assented to by the entire room, except for Angelina, who wanted to know how you could be certain that the money meant to save the Burmese child would not go anywhere else.

I probed further. "You all know Coke boy," I began. This was a young child who had been rescued after days in the rubble and whose first words were, "I want a Coke, with ice." He had become the darling of the nation. "Now suppose you could either spend the money to get this boy a Coke or save the life of a Burmese child."

Everyone was silent for a while until Angelina blurted out, "If we could be certain the money would go to save the life, then obviously it should be sent to save the life."

"Then it seems there is some obligation to help those in other nations, even in the midst of your own tragedy."

"Obviously," said Marlene, "our own needs must come first. But once these are adequately taken care of, yes, it seems there is some moral obligation to other nations."

"Yes, it is like Rousseau says," began Lionel. "If we see suffering, there is a natural tendency to help. Right now the suffering is in China, and that is why other nations are helping. But the same rule applies everywhere."

Given the pessimistic conclusions of the original *New York Times* editorial, I did not want to push this much more. I was happy to get any level of admission of moral obligation to other nations, even the tiniest. I would let them ponder what the proper middle ground between a life and a Coke should be.

I shifted the discussion to our personal obligation in disaster situations. What was our own obligation at this time?

"To do what we can."

"But how far do you go?"

This was the question on everyone's mind. Without a strong tradition of private charity or volunteerism—hence the difficulty in explaining to people what exactly I was doing in their country—China suddenly found itself awash in both. It is interesting to speculate on the reason for this historical lack. The economic conditions that prevailed until very recently are no doubt part of the explanation. The act of giving implies that one at first have enough for oneself, and this hasn't been the case throughout much of the country until the relatively recent past. But it is interesting to note that of the five relationships in classic Confucianism, three involve the obligation among family members, one concerns the bond between friends, and one involves the reciprocal duty between ruler and citizen. Left out is the connection among citizens that would form the philosophical basis for charity and volunteerism.

But whatever the historical precedent, the situation was different today. On my campus, donation bins were overflowing with clothes and blankets—the only things that were being accepted—while long lines formed in front of buildings that were collecting blood. More interesting was the spectacle—played out again and again on television—of numerous companies and organization parading their employees and managers across a stage in order that they might deposit cold, hard cash into a donation box. Just as Thomas wanted proof that this truly was the risen Christ and so insisted on sticking his fingers into the wounds, so

China, it seemed, needed to be guaranteed this really was a collective effort by having the entire nation play "show me the money."

But the most bizarre thing—at least from an American perspective—were the stories of prominent businessmen competing with each other to see who could commandeer the most vehicles and bring the greatest number of supplies to a disaster area. It would be as if Bill Gates himself showed up in New Orleans with a fleet of trucks filled with water while across town Steve Jobs set up a tent city (although given how things worked out there, this might not have been such a bad idea).

The resources of those gathered for this meeting, however, were much more limited. What degree of these resources should be expended toward this disaster?

Pioneer, who was more talkative than usual, started us off.

"One must avoid extremes," he said.

"What do you mean?" I asked.

"There was one teacher who, during the earthquake, completely deserted his students to save himself. There was another who went into the school to rescue fifteen children but lost his own life. Now his family has no father. Both of these seem wrong."

I thought about this for a moment. Although we would all view the former action as cowardly, there is in the Christian West an intellectual justification for the latter behavior. The biblical prescription is to "love thy neighbor as thyself," along with the claim in John 15:13 that there is no greater love than to sacrifice yourself for a fellow man—and while we can certainly debate the scope of this prescription, the Christian notion of *agape* requires, I think, a rather broad interpretation about exactly how far one's obligation extends. This goes a long way toward explaining how Americans can view running into a burning building with no thought for their own safety as heroic. By the same token, judging this action the height of foolishness, as my Chinese students had just done, likewise has a philosophical basis, in this instance, the Confucian notion of obligation to one's family as primary. In truth, I was not sure either side had a slam dunk case.

After discussing the sorts of actions they could engage in that were in line with this middle way view of obligation, I asked, "What about those who failed their obligation to society? It seems a lot of buildings were very badly built and that this is what caused a lot of the deaths."

"Yes," said a young woman, new or fairly new to the group. "In many places, the government buildings were left standing, while the schools were destroyed."

This was well reported, even in the Chinese press, so I did not think I was bringing up anything controversial. Still, the young man who had been so vehement at the start of the discussion offered a novel explanation for the different collapse rates, arguing that since schools were designed with larger rooms than government buildings, the former were structurally weaker and hence less able to withstand stress.

Thankfully, he was shouted down almost immediately. Still, I could sense no desire to go after those who had constructed the shoddy buildings, probably because the government was also discouraging the notion of retribution. The line in the press that was reflected here tonight was forward-looking: this tragedy could be a stepping stone to the enforcement of a building code that would prevent such tragedies in the future.

It was getting late. For obvious reasons, everyone was tired and seemed to want to take something positive from this discussion. I was willing to let them, but Pioneer would close things out a less than optimistic note. "I am not so sure if any good will come of this," he said and shook his head. "I think." He paused, as if searching for the right word. "I think corruption is China's national disease."

I did not know whether to take the group's silence as an indication that his contrarian view was beyond contempt or obviously correct. But it would have to be the last word.

TWENTY-FOUR

One Year Later: Chinese Sex Parks, Swine Flu, and My Return to Chengdu

I am sitting next to a large, young Chinese man who is wearing nothing but a pair of boxer shorts. We are both squatting on stools that reach no more than one foot off the floor and are situated around a small, rectangular table of corresponding height. It is lunchtime. There are a variety of Chinese dishes placed on the table, mostly vegetables, some with a little meat: steamed *nangua* (pumpkin), chunks of extremely fatty pork with green beans, bitter melon and beef, some nondescript greens. Of course, there is a big bowl of rice as well. Soup will be brought out later. It is a typical Chinese meal. Indeed, if there were a Chinese Norman Rockwell, this is the sort of thing he would paint, though I'm pretty sure he would leave out the kid in his underwear.

This is the third day of my return to Chengdu nearly a year after leaving, and things are not going as planned. My sumo-sized lunch companion is the least of my concerns. The fact that in the seventy-two hours I have been here he has neither left the house nor changed his shorts is more of a curiosity than anything else. The whole situation is more troubling to his mother, my friend Li Juan, at whose apartment I am staying while I am in Chengdu. Since deciding not to take the national college entrance exam several years ago, her son Feng Leng has split his time between writing an online novel and mastering the video game Grand Theft Auto, pursuing both tasks at a casual pace and, if the last three days are any indication, in casual attire. I don't know how the former project is coming along, but watching him play GTA on his mother's oversized television has led me to conclude that at least some of his energy is being put to good use.

In any case, I am not so concerned about large objects one can't miss as I am about microscopic entities invisible to the naked eye; in particular, the swine flu. Or, to be more precise, the paranoia with which the threat of the aforementioned virus is being greeted in China. While the rest of the world has delegated the H1N1 virus to the status of a minor inconvenience, China is in a state of high alert as I arrive. It all started about a week before I departed from the States, when the first confirmed Chinese case of swine flu turned up in, of all places, Chengdu. The joke now making the rounds is that the stricken young man, who initially stopped in Tokyo before arriving in Beijing and heading ultimately to Chengdu, is to be commended for his patriotism, for he first infected the Japanese and then reported his success to the leaders in Beijing. If you know anything about the Chinese attitude toward the Japanese, you will realize that, like many jokes, there is more than a grain of truth in the sentiment expressed in this claim. The irony of the whole situation is not lost on the Chinese either. Whereas a year ago, the Sichuan earthquake drove people to stay outdoors, the swine flu outbreak is lending a similar immediacy to remaining inside.

With the appearance of more cases across the country and the designation of pandemic status by the World Health Organization, Chinese attitudes changed dramatically and (despite the fact that the outbreak started in Mexico and citizens from all nations are infected) quickly shifted toward anti-Americanism. Why, I am asked again and again, are Americans traveling recklessly around the world and mindlessly infecting people from countries with much less-advanced health care systems? It might be my imagination as well, but Americans seem to be under special scrutiny. Days after I arrive, a U.S. citizen whose temperature is a whopping 98.9 is quarantined for three days on the suspicion that he might have the virus. Soon thereafter, the mayor of New Orleans, Ray Nagin, is shut away in Shanghai for a similar stretch simply because someone near him on the plane exhibited flu-like symptoms, while a group of visiting school children from New England is sequestered for six of their seven days in China even though none of them actually tested positive for the disease. Things get to the point where the U.S. State Department sends out a memo to travelers elaborating the random nature of the selection process for quarantine as well as the unsanitary conditions under which some people are held, suggesting that U.S. citizens seriously consider vacationing elsewhere, or at least purchasing travel insurance and bringing along a couple of big, thick books just in case. I am reminded of the scene in the movie *Blazing Saddles* where a criminal and his horse are both positioned on the gallows with nooses around their necks. Here, too, the notion of collective responsibility seems to have gotten out of hand. The Chinese, however, are making no apologies. Indeed, the whole thing strikes me as a sort of payback for the SARS epidemic of a few years ago, when China was made out to be the pariah of the international community for its ineffective measures against that illness.

But it is not the fear of quarantine that concerns me, at least for right now. My immediate worry is that the irrational attitude being exhibited toward a relatively harmless virus might threaten one of the main reasons for my journey. Although a large part of the rationale for returning to Chengdu was to check up on how students, friends, and colleagues are doing a year later, I have also been invited to moderate a session of the philosophy discussion group which, to my surprise and delight, is still up and running. However, it now seems a real possibility that the paranoia over the swine flu will cause students to miss the meeting despite the fact that I have been away from the United States for well past the time when I could infect anyone. Lionel, who has taken over control of the group, has hinted as much in the masterfully indirect and face-saving manner that is so characteristic of the Chinese. "Please do not be disappointed if not too many students come tonight," he writes me in an e-mail. "It is the Dragon Boat Festival and many students may have gone on vacation."

Commemorating the sacrifice of the patriotic poet Qu Yuan during the Warring States period, the holiday had recently been reinstated by the communist government in an attempt to integrate elements of traditional Chinese culture into society. So, it sounds like a plausible enough story. Until, that is, I check it out with a couple of other sources and discover that in all likelihood none of the students would have gone home, since this short two-day break occurs with tests looming near the end of the semester. Besides, the holiday does not actually take place until the day after our scheduled meeting. The bottom line is that if anyone is going to miss the discussion, it will probably not be for a celebratory reason.

The lack of attendance for the discussion group may not be such a problem, however, as the subject matter for the evening seems to have imploded anyway. In addition to suggesting I moderate a session of the philosophy club, Lionel has offered as well to let me choose the topic. As a result, I had been skimming the Internet for some current news story that would both spark interest and stir controversy. A headline announcing the impending opening of China's first sexually themed amusement park seemed made to order. Scheduled to begin business in October in Chongqing, the site was reported to contain such displays as a giant revolving model of a woman's legs and lower torso, clad only in an unflattering crimson thong, and an oversized replica of a set of genitals. The articles I had read hinted at a definite split in public attitudes toward this undertaking. Whereas some claimed that by providing sex education the park would help adults have a harmonious sex life, others worried that a sex-themed park signaled the decline of sexual morality. The brewing controversy portended well for a lively discussion.

Hence, it was with high hopes I went online shortly after settling in at my friend Li Juan's and did a Google search to check the latest developments. At first, I thought I had misread the results. It was not until I started clicking the links and scanning a couple of stories that it completely registered. Three days before our discussion group was set to meet, the government had ordered the closure of the park. "An investigation determined the park's content was vulgar and that it was neither healthy nor educational. It had had an evil influence on society and had to be torn down immediately," a municipal publicity official told the *Global Times* newspaper. In light of the government action, I had about as much chance of generating debate over the park as Li Juan did of having her son suddenly don a three-piece suit. As I finished lunch, my main thought was that no one was going to attend a discussion I had travelled six thousand miles to moderate, and even if someone did show up, there would not be anything to talk about. Just when I thought it couldn't get any worse, Li Juan informed me that her mother—who had eaten dinner with us the previous evening—had come down with a fever. And you probably won't need three guesses to figure out who was being pointed to as the most likely source of the infection. Perhaps I had more to worry than I realized from Feng Leng, who was probably quite fond of his grandmother.

I found myself reflecting back two years to that first session that I thought would never materialize and recalled the story of the farmer who loses his horse. Good news, bad news, who can tell? In this case, too, my fear turned out to be greatly overblown. Indeed, I take it as a testimony to the Chinese spirit of friendship that the students put aside what I knew were real concerns that they were meeting with a carrier of the deadly swine flu in order to see a former teacher who had travelled a long way to spend some time with them. Still, I did not hold out high hopes for a spirited discussion about the fate of the sex park. Just as not a single student had voiced doubts about the justification of the army crackdown in Tibet a little more than a year ago, I suspected that everyone tonight would similarly agree that the government had acted correctly.

While in the course of two years I was able to generate a good deal of controversy on everything from free will to free love, I soon discovered there was a limit to how far the envelope can be pushed in an authoritarian society. Although I understood their unwillingness to criticize their government's action on this (or any) topic in front of a group containing several foreigners (or anybody, for that matter), it did not prevent me from, in the best philosophical spirit, pressing them on their rationale for the lockstep agreement in this instance.

"China is very culturally conservative," began Marlene. "Sex is culturally taboo. It should come as no surprise that the park was not allowed to open."

In reply, I noted Chinese sex researcher Li Yinhe had recently been quoted as saying that in ancient times the Chinese people possessed more positive attitudes toward sexuality.

"Well," replied Marlene, "I do not know the historical situation. I was referring to the recent past."

"Let's talk about the recent past then," I countered. "Also according to Li Yinhe, since the 1980s, China has been gradually becoming a more sexually liberal society. One statistic she cites is that in Beijing, the percentage of people having premarital sex rose from under 16 percent in 1989 to over 60 percent in 2004. She believes, and I quote, 'The fact that the park has been built shows the change and that open attitudes to sex are now mainstream.' What do you think about that?"

"I am not so sure," said Lionel. "As you know, her views are considered to be somewhat controversial."

"Do you dispute the statistics?" I asked.

Richard, the retired hospice worker from California who was one of the few Westerners to attend the discussion on a regular basis, had showed up tonight after missing most of the sessions this past year. "Isn't it just the case that as a nation's economy develops its sexual attitudes become more liberal?"

However, neither Lionel nor Marlene (or anyone else for that matter) was ready to abandon the mantle of conservatism in their description of Chinese sexual attitudes.

"Perhaps in the past people were 'doing it' but not talking about it as much," offered up my old colleague Jiali, who had put in an appearance as well. "This would account for the difference in statistics."

"Even if sexual activity has increased, that doesn't necessarily mean the traditional values have changed," added Marlene. "The increase could come from couples in a committed relationship. And that would be consistent with a relatively conservative attitude."

Still, I wanted to say there were some ways in which Li Yinhe seemed correct in claiming that China was becoming a more sexually liberal society. I mentioned how surprised I had been early on in my time in China to discover the percentage of students who did not object to homosexuality. And I reminded them about our discussion of the transgendered, in which there was almost universal acceptance of this phenomenon. "I can't imagine your parents thinking the same thing in either of these matters."

"Yes," said Lionel. "This is one of the ways that our attitudes are different from our parents' generation."

Kristin, my old sitemate, jumped in here. "But how different are you really, Lionel? For example, what do you think about a woman who has more than one boyfriend?"

"I don't think it is looked on very favorably," he replied.

"By your parents' generation or by yours?"

"Both."

Here, Angelina stepped in with the story of a friend of hers whose multiple boyfriends might have earned her a reputation as a rebel by Western standards. In her hometown in China, she was a pariah. "She is considered," said Angelina, "I don't know the English, but anyway, she is a disgrace to her family."

"What do you think?" I asked.

"I do not approve of her behavior. Not because I think it is wrong to sleep around, but because she is ruining her chances for marriage."

"Sounds like she has a lot of chances for marriage," I replied.

"None of those men is going to marry her," said Lionel.

"How can you be so sure?"

"He is right," added Angelina.

"Again, how can you be so certain?"

She glanced around the room, looking for someone to help her out. And then, as had often been the case over the course of two years, she stepped up to deliver the blunt truth, "Because Chinese men want to marry a virgin."

For some reason I was taken aback by this. There were six young Chinese guys in the room and I quizzed each of them on the accuracy of this statement. Although a few were a bit embarrassed—and one needed to have the term translated—in the end they all assented to the proposition.

"So," I said, "it is OK for the guys to have sex with Angelina's friend and not hurt their chances of marriage, but not for Angelina's friend to sleep with them?"

No one disagreed. But in response Lionel asked, "What about in America?"

"Sure," I said. "There are sexual double standards in America. But except for my Mormon students, I would guess most young Americans don't expect to marry a virgin."

"Why would they want to?" added Richard. "Can you imagine the pressure?"

"Well, maybe," I said, trying to bring the conversation back to the original subject, "if they went to the sex theme park, there would not be so much pressure."

Since it was a rather lame transition, I was unsurprised that no one responded. I knew asking the group in general for a response was not going to get the ball rolling. So, as was often the case in the past, I picked on someone in particular.

"Lionel, you never told us what you think about the sex theme park. Should it have been shut down?"

"I think it is a good idea to educate the public about sexuality."

"But?" I asked, because I could feel a "but" coming on.

"But I think the owner is interested in making money, not in educating the public."

It was a classic on the one hand/on the other hand reply, typically Chinese and demonstrating a grace toward the opposition that is so often missing in American discussions. It was also an answer that harkened back to the old socialist (and, for that matter, Platonic) theory—certainly the view during the Cultural Revolution—that art ought to promote social well-being and not just be engaged in for its own sake. Lionel here seemed to be implying the same with business: it, too, ought to serve a social goal, and profit alone is not enough to justify it. I asked him if this is what he meant and when he said yes I pressed him further. "But what's wrong with making money? Isn't it a glorious thing to be rich?"

Everyone laughed, remembering how I'd beat that Deng Xiaoping quote to death over the course of two years. Pioneer, the philosophy graduate student, entered the conversation at this point. "Yes. It is a glorious thing to be rich. But Deng Xiaoping said it was only glorious if it truly helps China."

"Doesn't sex education help China?"

"I agree with Lionel," he replied. "I do not think the park is truly about sex education."

At the mention of sex education Kristin's ears perked up. She wanted to know exactly how the students here learned about sex.

A young man I didn't recognize said, "The Internet is our teacher."

Everyone laughed, but it was one of those nervous laughs that signals both the unpleasantness and the truth of what has just been said.

"Did any of your parents talk to you about sex?" she asked.

Silence.

"What about at school?"

"In my middle-school class, they told us that the more we knew about sex, the more likely we were to commit rape," said the young man who made the Internet comment. Everyone had a similar story of shortened lectures or no lectures at all. One of Kristin's female students said that in her class, only the boys were instructed on the topic.

Lionel weighed in. "I think there are two reasons why we are not provided with good sex education. Parents think the only thing we should be interested in is our academic studies. And our teachers believe that knowledge about sex is harmful." He continued in an almost pleading fashion. "We need direction in this area, and by 'we' I mean young people. This is what we are not getting." Perhaps I had been wrong about their unwillingness to criticize a government practice.

Marlene added that the situation is especially bad in the countryside. She related a story, immediately vouched for by others, about a rural couple who had gone to see a doctor because the wife was not pregnant. The problem, it seems, was that the newlyweds did not realize that sleeping in the same bed was not enough to do the trick. Although I suspected the tale to be more urban legend than hard news, it seemed to convey the spirit of the room tonight: China had a long way to go on the subject of sex education.

"How is sex education carried out in America?" Kristin's student pressed.

Kristin and I looked at each other. But before we could decide who should go first another newcomer to the group spoke up, a Chinese undergraduate who had just completed his freshman year at a university in Kentucky. He related how in his first week in the dorms, their class had been given a lecture about the importance of respecting the sexual needs of their roommates. For example, if the roommate had a boyfriend or girlfriend, they needed to negotiate with each other so that the couple could have time alone. From the looks on the students' faces tonight, you would have thought he had declared that he had received instruction on how to light his roommate on fire.

"So," I asked the group, trying to shake them from their state of shock. "Do you think that this will ever happen at Sichuan Normal?"

"Not with eight people in a dorm room," Marlene replied. I hadn't thought of that.

This prompted the Peace Corps China director, who had put in an appearance tonight, to relate how more than three decades earlier her class had been responsible for the integration of the dorms at the University of Washington.

"So," I riffed off that revelation, "do you all think that in thirty years China will have men and women in the same dorms?" In the spirit I had often seen of not dismissing a crazy idea for fear of offending its originator, Lionel replied, "I do not think so. But anything is possible."

The verdict this evening was that there had to be a middle way between the neglect typical of sex education in China and the overkill the subject receives in America. Like the nuanced on the one hand/on the other hand answers, middle way replies seem particularly Chinese, and in the two years I spent in the country I grew increasingly fond of this tone of moderation, in part because it struck me as so different from the confrontational extremism that is all too common in American discourse.

I wanted to probe this issue of changing sexual morality in China and the degree to which the sex theme park might be a symptom of this. However, it was getting late, and loud. The one drawback to the café was the karaoke place right below it. I suddenly remembered how by 8 p.m., even with the windows closed, it would become next to impossible to have a conversation without shouting. A new twist, however, was added tonight. Because of the Dragon Boat Festival, people were lighting off fireworks. As the screech and bang of the explosives mixed with the off-key screaming of the crooners below, I decided to throw in the towel after a few attempts to continue the discussion amidst the cacophony.

This time, it was Richard who had the last word. Noticing my frustration at having to halt the proceedings earlier than I had expected, he consoled me with, "Hey, how often do you get fireworks when talking about sex?"

TWENTY-FIVE

Final Thoughts: The Tao of Angelina

When I returned to Chengdu almost a year after completing my Peace Corps service, I made sure to set aside some time to meet separately with a half dozen of my favorite students in order to check in on how they were doing with their lives. I was especially interested in the three who were graduating. What path had they chosen for the next big step on their journeys? Interestingly, among them the trio had opted for the three most common routes for a Chinese undergraduate. Marlene was registered for graduate school in Chongqing, Angelina had accepted an offer to teach high school in nearby Mianyang, and adventurous Sophie had set off for Shanghai in order to break into the world of business.

Actually, Angelina's first choice had been to attend graduate school in teaching Chinese to foreigners. However, her interview in Xian did not go so well. She told me this with some sadness as we sat at the Pizza Hut in a mall in Chengdu—the very same one I had been about to enter when the earthquake hit. It went like this, she said. Wishing to impress on her that the Chinese language cannot be taught separately from the central concepts it is used to express, her examiners had asked her how she would explain the notion of Tao to someone studying under her. She froze, she said, and did not give a very good answer. If I had been running the discussion group this past year, things might have turned out differently, she added, since I was constantly emphasizing such cross-cultural comparisons.

Although I was of course saddened by her failure, I was heartened by the fact that her examiners shared my view about China, namely, that one cannot understand anything fundamental about the place—not the culture, the economy, the politics, or even the language—without coming to grips with its philosophy. For years I had made the same claim about the ancient Greeks to my students, declaring to their puzzled visages that one cannot even hope to appreciate something as basic as Greek architecture without understanding Homer. For proof, I would offer the Temple to Poseidon at Cape Sounion. Sitting on a cliff overlooking the Aegean on the outskirts of Athens, it is visited by tourists who come to watch one of the most memorable sunsets they will ever see in their lives. As the sun sinks into the water, the crowd invariably ceases their collective conversations and a quiet descends that reminds one of nothing so much as a church before the service commences. To all but the most obtuse observer, this silence before the sea is evidence that this world itself can be sacred; indeed, nothing can be more sacred.

Neither the location of a building dedicated to the god of the sea nor the emotion it evokes is an accident. Rather, these things spring from a philosophy that is at the heart of the Greek worldview. In one of the most famous scenes from the work that constitutes one half of the Greek bible, the *Odyssey*, Odysseus visits Hades in order to speak with the dead Achilles, who tells his former friend that he would rather be the lowest slave on earth than king of the underworld. The belief that, to the extent there is an afterlife, it is a pale imitation of this one runs counter to our Judeo-Christian tradition, which sees the next world as superior in the same way that the spiritual is vastly more significant than the material. But this view itself has architectural implications. Because material reality is unimportant, the Christian can put a church or cathedral anywhere, since what matters is the spiritual relation, not the geographical location. But if there is no greater reality than the physical, the actual setting of religious shrines becomes of the utmost importance. As in real estate, three things matter for a Greek temple: location, location, location. Hence, it is the philosophical belief that drives the architectural decision, or perhaps it's more correct to say the architecture is an expression of an underlying philosophy. In either case, the two are inextricably intertwined.

For the ancient Greeks, the entire meaning of life—including the sense of the sacred—is contained within this world. Many in the contemporary West who hear this tend to think that the result of accepting this perspective on reality is relativism or nihilism: the notion that if this world is all we have, then anything goes. Or, as Dostoevsky put it, if God is dead, then anything is permitted. But far from descending into the *Lord of the Flies*, the ancient Greeks gave us the Olympics, democracy, philosophy, the West's first great literature, and extra-virgin olive oil. I bring up the Greeks because it is through them that we can begin to answer Angelina's question. To restate an insight suggested earlier in the book, if we want to begin to understand China, we would be well advised to do so by using terms and a tradition that are already familiar to us. The ancient Greeks can serve as our touchstone in this endeavor.

Although both the ancient Greeks and modern Chinese recognize divine beings and powers, these entities play no role in the daily lives of the people. Practically speaking, this world is all that exists. I will refer to this as a de facto materialism. The Greeks, of course, had their pantheon of gods, led by Zeus. But perhaps because of their generally atrocious behavior, these immortals never served as standards for human conduct as, say, Jesus does for Christianity. Instead, the Greek gods were sought out most often to invoke a curse on a fellow citizen or pray for a benefit to befall one's self or family. Although China is nominally atheistic, Buddhist and Taoist temples abound and are quite popular. But for the most part, attendance at these temples plays the same role as worship of the Olympian pantheon did in ancient Greece. That is, it occurs primarily as the vehicle to either seek out or express gratitude for divine intervention.

Since for the ancient Greeks and modern Chinese this world is all we have and there is no immortal soul to be punished or rewarded, it comes as no surprise that egoism becomes the dominant ethical philosophy in both traditions. The great Greek scholar Gregory Vlastos summarizes the Greek attitude on this topic with the claim that all ancient Greek ethical thinking is eudaemonistic, meaning that the rational end for all our actions is the achievement of our own happiness. Both Confucianism and Taoism concur, albeit in radically different ways. For the Confucian, it is the project of self-cultivation that is the primary focus of all energy and effort, while the Taoist seeks what we might call a path of personal liberation and freedom. For neither the Greeks nor Chinese is the notion of carrying out the will of heaven to the detriment of one's own well-being (e.g., sacrificing your son because some disembodied voice suggested it would be a good idea) or of spending one's resources to assist a stranger (à la the Good

Samaritan) seen as a particularly wise strategy. Instead, a healthy self-interest predominates so that if one does engage in apparent altruism, it is inevitably carried out for the purposes of increasing personal power or with the belief that it will benefit one in the long run (e.g., guanxi).

A de facto materialism and egoism may seem the worst possible combination. If all that exists, practically speaking, is this world, and we ought to maximize our self-interest, what is to prevent one from behaving like Attila the Hun? Or Donald Trump? In fact, far from entailing nihilism, the notion for both the ancient Greeks and modern China is that there exist real ethical standards that can direct human behavior. Although this seems not only counterintuitive but downright contradictory, in fact, the existence of regulating norms that restrict action is just as logical a conclusion to draw from materialism and egoism as is an "anything goes" philosophy. Consider the case of physical health. With respect to issues involving the body, there obviously exists only material reality, and just as clearly, unless we are masochists, we are out to maximize our well-being in this area. But this does not mean we adopt an "anything goes" philosophy with respect to our bodies. Instead, we recognize the existence of real laws with real consequences. For example, if we want to achieve physical well-being, it's a good idea to exercise regularly and watch what we eat. Conversely, a steady diet of donuts, potato chips, and channel surfing is apt to have deleterious effects in this area. Since patterns and regularities exist with respect to the human body, the intelligent person discovers these laws and follows them. The same seems to hold true in the case of psychological well-being. Like the profession of medicine, psychology offers its own list of illnesses and disorders—as well as a real standard of psychological health—without making any assumptions about the existence of a spiritual reality. Again, the intelligent person tries to put his or her life in line with these laws of human behavior.

So, if the existence of laws in the physical and psychological realms does not require the presence of a spiritual reality, it should come as no surprise that for both the ancient Greeks and modern Chinese, the fact that there is only the natural world does not preclude the presence of a moral law. Indeed, in both traditions ethical laws for regulating human conduct have the same status as laws of physical and psychological health: they are real and relevant and are sought out by the intelligent person wishing to live a good life. One discovers them in the same way one discovers the laws in the other two areas—through observation, reflection, and experience. Perhaps the most famous of these moral laws is known as the middle way or doctrine of moderation. Aristotle tells us that with respect to our health, excess and deficiency are detrimental, as we can plainly see is the case with food, drink, and exercise. Instead, when it comes to physical well-being, moderation is the key. The same holds true, he argues, with respect to virtue. The man who flees from everything is not virtuous but a coward, and the man who flees from nothing is foolish and not brave. Like all virtue, courage involves a middle path between the extremes.

Not surprisingly, we find the same doctrine of moderation in both Confucian and Taoist thought. Although the word for "middle way" appears only once in *The Analects of Confucius*, the term itself is both the title and the central theme for one of the four classics of Confucian thought, *The Doctrine of the Mean*. Similarly, the *Tao Te Ching* echoes the doctrine of moderation, warning about the effects of extreme behavior with such claims as, "A strong wind does not last all morning," and "He who rushes ahead doesn't go far."[1] In this way, these admonitions reflect perfectly the words etched above another Greek shrine, the Temple of Delphi: "Nothing in excess."

This, then, is how I would begin to answer Angelina's question, by stating that the Tao is neither arbitrary in the sense that it is not made by humans and so cannot be altered by them, nor is it absolute in that it does not exist separately from physical reality in a spiritual realm. Rather the Tao, whose rules such as the doctrine of moderation and avoidance of extremes can be derived from observation of nature, provides a guide for an effective and fulfilling human life. In this way, it plays the same role in the moral realm as the laws of physical health do with respect to our bodies. Of course, Angelina would not have been wrong to simply quote the first sentence from the *Tao Te Ching*: "The Tao that can be spoken of is the not the eternal Tao" (although that probably would not have helped her with her examiners either).

The three claims just discussed (materialism, egoism, and ethical naturalism) certainly pervade this book to the degree that almost without exception they are shared by the students and help to define their worldviews. In addition, I would argue that these theses constitute a useful prism through which to view contemporary China. This might at first only seem to confirm the widely held belief in the strangeness or otherness of the country—one of the issues I struggled with during my two years. A de facto materialist nation of egoists with an ethical system derived from nature could not, it seems, be more different from a country in which 90 percent of citizens believe in a God who is the source of moral law, one of which is to love thy neighbor as thyself. But as I have just finished explaining, the ancient Greeks, who are as definitive an influence on Western civilization as exists, accepted the same three theses that serve as the foundation for Chinese thought. Hence, any peculiarity we assign to China based on these three claims would seem to result in the "I'm rubber, you're glue" effect. That is, in accusing China of intellectual strangeness, we demonstrate nothing so much as a lack of self-knowledge.

Consider the case of human rights. While there is no single Chinese position on human rights, language that is often heard in popular media invariably involves a disdain for the "Western conception of human rights." Although this may sound like an alternate notion of human rights is presupposed—perhaps a "Chinese conception" that is as inflexible and as metaphysically anchored as its Western counterpart—in fact, the ensuing comments invariably reveal nothing of the sort is intended. So, for example, on a recent political discussion, a CCTV9 (the English-language Chinese station) commentator opined, to the approval of the Chinese panel, that when it comes to human rights, "no country or nation should think that it possesses the truth." That these same words were offered up by Lionel in one of our discussions more than a year before is not, I submit, a coincidence. Rather, this skepticism is underpinned by an ancient philosophical tradition—the notion that the doctrine of moderation counsels epistemic modesty as well. That is, if the Tao itself is unknowable, so is anything as profound as human rights. Aristotle made precisely the same point in the *Ethics* when he declared we should expect no more precision in an area than it is able to give us and, to paraphrase, ethics and politics ain't math.

Hence, I would suggest that the hope that China is going to suddenly or even eventually accept a Western-style doctrine of human rights is not only unsupported by any evidence but runs counter to the basic philosophical underpinnings of the society. This does not mean that there may not be other ways to bring about essentially the same results as are achieved by rights in the Western tradition. Some scholars, for instance, have recently argued that Confucianism can serve as a grounding for such claims. However, it does imply that invoking the vocabulary of human rights in East-West dialogue may not be the most fruitful strategy to follow if one wishes to engage in a serious discussion of the subject.

Other situations involving a connection between ancient thought and modern actions come to mind. For example, the corruption that caused so many school buildings to collapse during the Sichuan earthquake or the toxic dumping that is resulting in astounding cancer rates in some villages do not so much seem the result of a philosophical worldview as evidence of a failure to apply one. That is, it is not clear that these scenarios represent a deficiency of the Confucian moral view any more than Bernie Madoff demonstrates the failure of the Judeo-Christian outlook. The moral basis for criticizing such actions already exists within the culture. Indeed, the popularity of Yu Dan's works is evidence of an active interest in these ancient ways. However, applying these principles on a widespread scale is obviously something of a work in progress, to say the kindest thing that can be said on this point.

In any case, I have not tried to lay out a grand theory of China. I doubt that such a one exists any more than there is a grand theory of America. Instead, I have presented one perspective through which to view contemporary China: the philosophical reflections of a group of undergraduates in Sichuan province over a two-year period. If any knowledge about China is to be garnered from this book, it is to come through paying attention to the words and wisdom of the students themselves. In her most recent book, *China Witness: Voices from a Silent Generation*, Xinran said "knowledge about China is so small, it is a decimal fraction many positions after the decimal point."[2] My only hope is that I have made some contribution, however small, to moving that decimal point a notch in the right direction.

NOTES

CHAPTER 2. WHAT IS THE GOOD LIFE?
1. Roger T. Ames and Henry Rosemont Jr., *The Analects of Confucius: A Philosophical Translation* (New York: Ballantine Books, 1998), 71.
2. Richard E. Nisbett, *The Geography of Thought: How Asians and Westerners Think Differently . . . and Why* (New York: Free Press, 2003), 37.
3. Ames and Rosemont, *Analects*, 99.
4. Ibid., 62.
5. Ibid., 92.

CHAPTER 4. WHAT IS A GOOD MARRIAGE?
1. Nisbett, *Geography*, 63.

CHAPTER 5. WHAT IS THE MEANING OF LIFE?
1. Ames and Rosemont, *Analects*, 76.
2. Ibid., 73.
3. Ibid., 37.
4. Roger T. Ames and David L. Hall, *Thinking Through Confucius* (Albany: State University of New York Press, 1987), 14.

CHAPTER 6. WHAT IS A HERO?
1. Nisbett, *Geography*, 170–71.
2. Ibid., 173–74.
3. Stephen Mitchell, *Tao Te Ching: A New English Version* (New York: Harper-Perennial, 1991), secs. 2, 22.

CHAPTER 7. FATE OR FREE WILL?
1. Lin Yutang, *My Country and My People* (Beijing: Foreign Language Teaching and Research Press, 2007), 194.
2. Nisbett, *Geography*, 87.

CHAPTER 9. WHAT IS A GOOD EDUCATION?
1. Nisbett, *Geography*, 48–49.

CHAPTER 10. WHAT IS HUMAN NATURE?
1. Martin Palmer, *The Book of Chuang Tzu* (New York: Penguin, 2007), 147.

CHAPTER 11. ARE THERE TWO SIDES TO EVERY COIN?
1. Mitchell, *Tao*, secs. 8, 1, 5.
2. Palmer, *Chaung Tzu*, 145.
3. Mitchell, *Tao*, sec. 2.

CHAPTER 12. IS MARRIAGE NECESSARY?
1. Xinran, *The Good Women of China: Hidden Voices* (New York: Anchor, 2003).

CHAPTER 14. WHAT IS THE DIFFERENCE BETWEEN EASTERN AND WESTERN THINKING?
1. Lin, *My Country*, 42–57.
2. Ibid., 77–90.
3. Nisbett, *Geography*, 65.

CHAPTER 15. WHAT IS THE VALUE OF THE PAST?
1. TNR Staff, "China's War on Christmas." *The New Republic: The Spine Blog.* http://www.tnr.com/blog/the-spine/chinas-war-christmas.
2. Zhou Bajun, "Delicate Balance needed when East meets West," *China Daily*, February 6, 2007.
3. Liu Shinan, "Improve knowledge of Chinese, other cultures," *China Daily*, December 27, 2006.

CHAPTER 17. WHAT ARE THE LIMITS OF PRIVACY?
1. For an overview of the Edison Chen case see, http://en.wikipedia.org/wiki/Edison_Chen_photo_scandal.

CHAPTER 25. FINAL THOUGHTS: THE TAO OF ANGELINA
1. Mitchell, *Tao*, secs. 23, 24.
2. Xinran, *China Witness: Voices from a Silent Generation* (New York: Pantheon, 2009), 203.

INDEX

ABOUT THE AUTHOR

PETER J. VERNEZZE has edited two books (*Bob Dylan and Philosophy*, *The Sopranos and Philosophy*) in the bestselling philosophy series, Open Court's "Popular Culture and Philosophy," and is the author of *Don't Worry, Be Stoic: Ancient Wisdom for Troubled Times*. He lives in Tucson, Arizona.

3 20